£1.50

D1149612

# Healthy Living
# YEARBOOK
get fit and enjoy it, in every season

dear Andrea,
enjoy getting into it!

# Tracy Griffen

Healthy Living Yearbook
First published in the United Kingdom in 2011 by
Tracy Griffen – Griffen Fitness Ltd
3 Balfour Street
Edinburgh
EH6 5BY

www.getfitandenjoyit.com

A catalogue record of this book is available from the British Library.

ISBN: 978-0-9570618-0-4

While substantial care and effort has been taken in the research of this book, Griffen Fitness Ltd cannot accept any responsibility for any errors, omissions or inaccuracies. If any are found please feel free to contact us.

Cover design and typesetting by Heather Macpherson, www.raspberryhmac.co.uk

# Contents

*For the lovely Andy, yin to my yang*

# Introduction

## A word of warning:
## This not a traditional fitness book

We all live with the seasons, whether we acknowledge it or not. I moved from sunny Australia to chilly Scotland fourteen years ago and had never encountered such a distinct seasonal cycle. As a Personal Trainer working with individuals on a one to one basis, it became apparent to me that we are all instinctively in tune with nature. No matter that most of us live in concrete jungles rather than open green spaces, we all benefit from working with the ebb and flow of the world around us.

Consequently this book is designed to be a seasonal guide. You can either read it from cover to cover, or dip into it depending on the month. If in doubt, check the index at the back. I hope to bring you ideas to inspire you to get active and eat well no matter the weather. All opinions in this yearbook are most definitely my own, and are based on extensive research and practical experience.

The following chapters contain oodles of ideas to get you moving. However, I believe you can best learn new exercises from a live human rather than a book, so if you're looking for a personalised programme, drop me a line. An exercise professional will guide you on good form, technique and breathing which are essential for safe and effective exercise. Please note that if you are new to exercising, take it easy and listen to your body.

I always appreciate questions and feedback, so please feel free to contact me. Full contact details are on page 178.

Wishing you all a happy and healthy year ahead,

Tracy

# JANUARY

The start to a new year is a great time to put in place new improved habits. We are all creatures of habit and if you can replace old behaviour patterns with new healthy ones, you can make positive changes to your lifestyle without feeling deprived. Here are some ideas to take you through the dark month of January.

## WHAT'S IN SEASON

**Beetroots, cabbages: red, white and green, celeriac, chicory, kohlrabi, Jerusalem artichoke, leeks, onions, potatoes, spinach and chard, the last of the apples and pears.**

It can feel difficult to eat seasonally mid-winter, but remember that you can use canned and frozen vegetables if you can't find decent fresh vegetables in the shops. Dried fruit and fruit juice can also count towards your five a day.

## OATCAKE TOPPING OF THE MONTH

In the middle of winter it's common to crave comfort food, so January's oatcake topping is a combination of comfort and nutrition: spread an oatcake with low fat cream cheese and sprinkle with chopped fresh parsley (a rich source of vitamin C, beta-carotene and folic acid). Parsley is also a natural breath freshener, so next time you have some as a garnish – eat it.

# Easy Winter Recipes

## Porridge

Porridge is the winter king of breakfasts and is very easy to make, either on the hob or in the microwave. Jumbo oats are best as they are whole and therefore have a lower GI. Avoid the powdery instant oat cereals as they have been highly processed.

Save time in the morning by pre-preparing your porridge the night before. Simply place ½ cup of porridge oats in a bowl / pan with a cup of water (or ½ water, ½ milk if you prefer). In the morning, simply heat and eat. You can also add goodies like dried cranberries, sunflower seeds or wheatgerm for gourmet porridge. It's a great way to start a chilly day.

## Carrot & Orange Soup

There's something very nice about a big bowl of soup in the middle of winter. This soup is loaded with goodness and is a cheery orange colour to boot, guaranteed to brighten up even the bleakest evening...

*Serves four*

  500g carrots
  30g butter
  125ml orange juice
  1.25l vegetable stock
  1 small onion, roughly chopped
  3 – 4 tsp fresh thyme (or 1 tsp dried)
  Freshly ground black pepper
  Natural yoghurt, for serving

★ Peel and slice the carrots. Place carrots and butter in a large heavy-based pan and cook on a medium heat for 10 minutes, stirring occasionally.

★ Add the orange juice, stock and onion. Bring to the boil, then add thyme and pepper.

★ Reduce heat; cover and cook for 20 minutes, or until the carrots are tender. Allow to cool.

★ Blend the mixture until smooth. Reheat soup and serve. Garnish with a dollop of natural yoghurt and a sprig of fresh thyme. You can also add a sprinkle of nutmeg or zest of orange for extra decoration.

# Easy Peasy Pea and Pearl Barley 'Risotto'

This is such a simple and cheap dish, no one can say that healthy eating is a tough thing to do. The cooking time is just under an hour and it needs minimal attention as it will not stick to the pan like traditional risotto. You can get in from work, pop it on the hob and get changed out of your work clothes as the pearl barley is cooking. Easy. It also keeps well for reheating the next day so is a good packed lunch option. Go to town with trying different herb variations and different cheeses.

*Makes four large servings*

2 tbsp butter
500g pearl barley, rinsed
1 vegetable stock cube
200g frozen peas
250g mushrooms, sliced
2 cloves garlic, crushed (optional)
Handful various chopped herbs, I like parsley, sage and thyme
150g mature cheddar cheese, grated

★ Melt 1 tbsp butter in a big pan.
★ Sauté the rinsed pearl barley to coat in butter for 2 – 3 minutes.
★ Add crumbled stock cube to 600ml boiling water and pour over pearl barley.
★ Cover and simmer on a medium heat for just over 30 minutes, top it up bit by bit with 800ml hot water until it's all absorbed.
★ When cooked, remove from heat and stir in the peas, cover and set aside for 10 minutes. Season with pepper. No salt is required thanks to the saltiness of the stock.
★ As you're doing this, sauté the mushrooms in the remaining butter.
★ Stir through cheese and mushrooms to serve. You can use more herbs as a garnish.

# Corny Fritters

*Serves four, or two people two meals*

150g dried polenta
40g plain flour
1 tsp bicarbonate of soda
500ml milk
300g corn kernels
1 tbsp melted butter
1 tbsp finely chopped spring onions
2 egg whites
1 tbsp coconut or olive oil
pepper and salt (optional)

★ Mix polenta, flour and bicarb in a big bowl with the milk.
★ Stir in corn, melted butter and spring onions.
★ Whisk egg whites until peaks form and gently fold into mixture (do this just before cooking).
★ In a heavy bottomed frying pan, heat the oil to a moderate heat.
★ Drop large spoonfuls of the mixture in and cook both sides until golden.

The batter keeps OK in the fridge if you'd like to save some for the next day.

# A Salad for Winter

*Serves two*

Jerusalem artichoke is not actually an artichoke but a winter root vegetable native to Peru. It has a mildly sweet, smoky flavour, crunchy texture and can be eaten raw or cooked. Be aware that it discolours when sliced, so pop the sliced root into a bowl of water with a squeeze of lemon until ready for use.

2 tbsp roasted pumpkin seeds
2 handfuls rocket, washed
1 little gem lettuce, washed and chopped
1 Jerusalem artichoke
½ lemon, juiced
Drizzle olive oil
1 tbsp balsamic vinegar

- ★ To roast the pumpkin seeds: heat them in a heavy bottomed saucepan on a medium heat. Agitate regularly or they will burn. Give the pan a shoogle when you see the seeds puffing up. Place aside in a bowl to cool.
- ★ Wash and chop the lettuce and combine with the rocket in a salad bowl.
- ★ Finely slice the Jerusalem artichoke and it place into a bowl of water with a dash of the squeezed lemon until time for serving.
- ★ In a small bottle or jar combine the rest of the lemon juice, balsamic vinegar and olive oil. Stopper the container and shake.
- ★ When the seeds have cooled down, add them to the salad.
- ★ Just prior to serving, add Jerusalem artichoke and toss salad to combine.
- ★ Serve with dressing on the side.

## Butter Bean Bake

*Serves two*

1 can butter beans, drained and rinsed
1 small jar of good quality pasta sauce
1 – 4 cloves garlic, chopped finely
1 small onion, chopped finely
Handful of sundried tomatoes, soaked if required
1 tsp olive oil
Handful of fresh basil, ripped

Serve with:
Brown rice
Sprinkle of rocket leaves
Wedge of lemon as garnish

- ★ Sauté the onion and garlic in a pan with the olive oil until golden.
- ★ Add the beans and the pasta sauce and stir through, heat through.
- ★ Take off the heat and stir through the sundried tomatoes and most of the basil.
- ★ Transfer mixture to a casserole dish and cook in a pre heated oven at 200°C for 20 – 30 minutes or until bubbling.
- ★ Serve over brown rice and garnish with a sprinkling of rocket and sprig of basil.

# Fabulous Flapjacks

Make a tray of a dozen flapjacks at the beginning of the week and you will have snacks for the week. These are healthier than shop bought snacks, as despite having sugar (brown) and fat (butter) in, they are all natural.

50g butter, melted

75g soft brown sugar or honey / agave syrup, to taste (you can add less)

1 free range organic egg (as happy hens lay better eggs)

1 tsp mixed spice

1 tsp baking powder

150g porridge oats

50g plain flour

50 – 100g raisins / dried cranberries / sunflower / pumpkin seeds / mixed nuts

1 dessertspoon of golden syrup (optional)

★ Preheat oven to 150°C.

★ In a bowl, mix butter and soft brown sugar. Add the egg and mix.

★ Weigh the plain flour straight into the bowl, add baking powder and mixed spice and mix.

★ Now add porridge oats and seeds / dried fruit, (I like sunflower seeds and dried cranberries). Mix well together. If you have any syrup, a dessertspoon here will ensure they stay soft and chewy but it's not vital.

★ They are now ready to cook. You can use 12 paper cupcake cases or simply spoon the mixture straight into a lightly greased muffin tray. Alternatively, you can use a baking tray, but wait until the flapjacks are completely cold before cutting them up.

★ Bake for around 15 minutes. They are nicer underdone rather than too crunchy.

★ Cool and wrap individually to take to work / school.

# Resisting Temptation Hints of the Month

## The Power of Positivity

New Year is a traditional time to kick start new healthy habits. The trick to 'resisting temptation' is for there not to be temptation in the first place. In other words, how you look at a 'temptation' is crucial as to whether you overcome it. For example, you wish to lose weight and cut out eating junk food, so it makes no sense if you 'hold onto' previous junk food beliefs. Which of the following statements do you think is more motivating?

"I would prefer to eat food that is nutritious and good for me, and chocolate biscuits aren't ticking those boxes"

or "I love chocolate biscuits, but I am not allowed to have them"?

Pretty obvious, eh?

So whilst you're setting out on your new healthy version of yourself, think about the frame of reference you give to 'temptations'. It could make all the difference.

## Your End of Week Routine

Is Friday after work your undoing? Many of us live for the weekend and when it arrives, undo the healthy living that we have been enjoying all week. If you know your trouble spot is Friday evening, change your routine.

If you usually go to the pub or open a celebratory bottle of wine when you get in the door, think about changing your habits. An after-work yoga class (Friday afternoon classes tend to be quiet), a swim or a walk home from the office can diffuse the urge to overindulge.

## Savour Your Pressies

The festive season can also be one of overindulgence, which can result in leftover boxes of Christmas chocolates, puddings and biscuits… Instead of eating them all to empty the cupboards, see how long you can make them last.

Can you make a box of chocolates last until Easter? An easy way to do that is to hide them at the top back of the cupboard behind healthy food.

# Fad or Fab

## Ab Wheel

The ab wheel is as it sounds – a wheel that works your abs. It looks like something from a toy box, and this piece of kit is pure retro. This is what folk used in gyms before Swiss balls were popular.

From a kneeling position hold onto the handles and push it away from your body. It's quite good fun, in a pushing a toy car kind of way, but if you have a weak lower back, you may find it a bit nippy. The wheel can only move back and forth, whereas a Swiss ball challenges your stability more as it can move laterally. Fun but definitely an old school fad that has become outdated.

## Compression Tights: Not Just for Grannies

Do you ever get 'dead' or tired legs? Compression hosiery has long been prescribed by doctors to those suffering varicose veins. Now some clever bod has discovered that compression technology is equally as useful to professional athletes. Compression clothing is designed to be skin tight, with graduated pressure from bottom to top to assist blood flow. This is especially effective in helping reduce fatigue in the legs if you have been exercising hard, or even on your feet all day. Paula Radcliffe has been seen wearing compression socks whilst marathon running.

They're a lot groovier than the compression stockings prescribed for varicose veins, and also much more comfortable. They're also a warm winter under-layer. For those who need quick leg recovery after a race or experience tired legs, these are fab.

# Exercise of the Month: Nordic Walking

Nordic Walking is basically walking with poles. To quote the UK Nordic Walking website www.nordicwalking.co.uk "Originating from summer training for cross-country skiers, Nordic Walking works your upper and lower body at the same time, strengthening your back, legs and arms, and reducing neck and shoulder tension – all this while improving the health of your heart and lungs." Try it with a qualified instructor, as there is a knack to how pushing off with the poles.

# January Articles

## All About Abdominals

You probably hear lots of talk about 'core strength'. What is it, and why is it so important for overall fitness? There are three main muscle groups to your abs, and you need to know where they are to understand how to exercise them.

Firstly, the **rectus abdominis** is a line of muscles that run down the front of your belly. Children of the eighties may recall Peter Andre's 'six pack' being on display. They're a superficial muscle group near the surface, and are responsible for flexing the spine (bringing the rib cage closer to the pelvis). They are used in abdominal crunching or sit up movements.

Your **internal and external obliques** are, as the names suggest, located on each side of your torso. They work in tandem to rotate the torso and stabilise the abdomen in twisting and side bend movements. Untoned obliques result in 'love handles'.

The last of the three, the **transversus abdominis** is shaped like a corset around your tummy, crossing over (transverse). It's a stabilising muscle group that keeps your insides in and keeps you upright. This is the muscle group that is important to exercise and strengthen, as it is a deep muscle group often not exercised in traditional methods that involve movement. Its function is to keep you stable, so many balancing and Pilates exercises focus on using this deep muscle to build core strength. Swiss ball exercises or anything that challenges your balance will assist.

You can work out what your transversus abdominis does by relaxing your tummy, then pulling your belly button into your spine. You may feel that your waist line is instantly reduced and certainly if you practise enough, you can lose inches from your waist just by knowing how to engage your deep abdominals… and your posture will thank you. You may even be able to help or prevent back pain, just by using your front muscles more.

By increasing core strength, you can also help your balance (as it's your core muscles that help to keep you upright), so from a practical point of view it is well worth doing. By exercising all three groups together you can work to improve your posture and get rid of belly bulge.

# Cholesterol: Sadly Misunderstood?

Who needs cholesterol in their body? We all do! Cholesterol has a number of useful functions. It helps protect cell membranes, it assists nerves to send messages and it helps our bodies build certain hormones. But there's an aspect of cholesterol that poses a health issue. To understand this, I need to explain how cholesterol moves about the body.

What is commonly referred to as cholesterol is actually a lipoprotein (fat + protein), a 'raft' that carries cholesterol around the body. There are a number of these lipoproteins that serve different purposes.

VLDL (Very Low Density Lipoproteins) carry cholesterol and fatty acids from the liver. They are then turned into LDL (Low Density Lipoproteins) as they lose fat and gain more cholesterol. These LDLs are then circulated around the body, dropping off cholesterol as they go. When they have offloaded all their cholesterol, they turn into HDL (High Density Lipoprotein).

VLDL and LDL ('bad cholesterols') are low in density and therefore squishy enough to permeate blood vessels and can eventually cause a blockage. The blockage of blood vessels is the whole issue of 'cholesterol'. HDL ('good cholesterols') are higher in density, 'harder' and therefore do not do this.

So do we need to eat cholesterol? No. Our liver produces all the cholesterol we need. The more we eat, the less it produces. The healthier option is to eat less food with cholesterol and let our liver get on with it.

Cholesterol is found only in animal products, and never in plant matter. So it is quite easy to work out which foods to cut back on to assist lowering cholesterol levels (actually VLDL and LDL levels).

**Eat less:** meat, poultry, egg yolks, full fat dairy products

**Eat more:** fruit, vegetables and wholegrain foods. Vegetarians rejoice. Omnivores choose lean meat and dairy.

And what else? Exercise. Keeping active also helps keep these levels in check. Sometimes cholesterol levels are genetic, and a healthy diet and active lifestyle can help normalise this.

# Too Much Pressure? All about High Blood Pressure

We all know that we have a measurable blood pressure, but have you ever stopped to think about exactly what your blood pressure means? What is your GP measuring when they place that nifty inflatable cuff on your arm and what relevance does it have to your well being?

Your heart pumps blood to all parts of your body through arteries. When your heart beats, a surge of blood is pushed through your arteries and the pressure against your artery walls is at its highest. This is called the systolic reading (the higher number of the two). When your heart is at rest between beats, this is the lowest pressure, or diastolic pressure.

Your blood pressure reading always shows both your systolic and diastolic blood pressure, the systolic (higher number) over the diastolic (lower number).

Your blood pressure varies throughout the day depending on your level of activity and / or emotions (i.e. nervousness temporarily increases blood pressure). An overall high blood pressure reading means that your heart has to do more work to get the same amount of blood to your extremities. Not only this, but your arteries have a harder time as there is more internal pressure on them. This can lead to the walls of your blood vessels thickening to deal with the increased pressure. A thickened blood vessel wall means less blood can get through. High blood pressure can lead to stroke, heart attack, heart failure or kidney failure.

Normal blood pressure is 130/85 or below, while up to 140/90 is called 'high normal' and anything above 140/90 is high (hypertension).

If you have high blood pressure or are keen to keep yours at a healthy level, there are a number of lifestyle aspects to consider:

**Salt:** Reduce the amount of sodium that you consume. Studies have shown that an increased consumption of salt leads to higher blood pressure in many individuals. Salt causes our body to retain more water. In turn this extra water in our blood vessels can increase blood pressure (as there is more liquid being pumped through). Excess salt can also damage kidneys, which remove sodium from the body.

Processed food is where the Western diet gets most of its salt. If you do eat supermarket packaged food, check the labels for the level of salt (sodium). Even better, eat fresh natural food and avoid pre-packaged meals.

A simple guideline is to avoid foods that contain more than 0.2 grams of sodium per 100 grams of food and choose foods that contain less than 0.1 grams of sodium per 100 grams. The aim is to reduce your intake to less than a teaspoon a day, which is the same as 2 grams of sodium.

It should also be noted that salt levels vary wildly from one brand to another. For example, Morrisons baked beans contain 3.2g of salt, that's over half of the recommended daily salt levels. Co-op and Heinz contain a more sensible 2.1g, which is just over a third of the daily salt levels. This example also illustrates that packaged food contains a disproportionately high level of salt.

As a personal note, when I first met my other half Andy, he ate microwave meals nearly every day – the life of a bachelor. We started cooking food together and he started eating freshly prepared food every night. After a year or so, he bought himself a microwave meal as a treat and couldn't eat it as it tasted too salty. Our tastes do adjust and you can make fresh food tasty using herbs, spices and lemon or lime juice.

**Exercise:** Getting regular exercise can help lower your blood pressure. Regular pulse raising activity exercises your heart, the most important muscle in your body. Many athletes have a low resting heart rate and low blood pressure as they regularly train their body to deliver oxygen more efficiently around their bodies, thereby moving more easily and breathing more effectively. Losing body fat is an effective way to lower your blood pressure.

**Alcohol:** High alcohol consumption (more than 14 units per week for women, 21 for men) can increase blood pressure. Increased alcohol consumption also usually leads to increased weight.

**Give up smoking:** A fairly obvious one…

**Cholesterol levels:** Cholesterol can build up in blood vessels and cause a restriction to the amount of blood that can be pumped through. If you have high cholesterol levels, a high blood pressure can prove fatal.

**Stress levels:** Do you have a stressful job? Or are you always worrying about something? High stress levels can lead to an increase in blood pressure. If you are feeling stressed for a large portion of the day, this may mean your blood pressure is elevated unduly. Try going for a walk at lunch, or try a yoga or mediation class. Hatha yoga is a great way to unwind and chill out.

By considering all of the above points and making some (sometimes small) changes to your lifestyle, you can lower your blood pressure and improve your quality of living.

# FEBRUARY

The darkest months are behind us... February is one of the coldest months but there's something rather good about the lengthening days. A clear crisp winter day makes perfect walking conditions so try a weekend walk in the country, but pack lots of warm clothes.

## WHAT'S IN SEASON

**Beetroot, Brussels sprouts, cabbage (white and red), carrots, cauliflower, chicory, celeriac, celery, chard, Jerusalem artichoke, kale, kohlrabi, leeks, mushrooms, onions, parsnips, potatoes, purple sprouting broccoli, salsify, spinach, squashes, swede and turnips.**

## OATCAKE TOPPING OF THE MONTH

It seems wholly appropriate that avocado, known as 'the fertility fruit' by the Aztecs, is the Valentine's oatcake topping of the month. Avocado is a very nutritionally 'complete' topping, a slow burning fuel packed full of minerals and vitamins, as well as good monosaturated fats.

Buy avocados hard and ripen them at home. They are ripe when their stalk wobbles and they give slightly to the touch. Slice them or mash them onto oatcakes with ground pepper or harissa, a piquant North African red pepper paste.

# Easy Winter Recipes

## Raw Food Ideas

We should all eat more food in its raw natural state. I can hear you thinking, "it's all very well to encourage people to eat more raw food, but how can this be done in the middle of winter when very little is in season?" Here's how:

★ Have some salad with each meal. It doesn't need to be much but a handful of rocket tossed on top of risotto or pasta enlivens the dish and adds valuable nutrients.

★ Sprinkle some sunflower seeds on top of your lunch.

★ Ripen an avocado yourself and make guacamole with freshly squeezed lemon juice and pepper. Tasty on pretty much anything.

★ Snack on a piece of fruit.

★ Juicing is another way of enjoying raw fruit and vegetables.

★ On the weekend, a bowl of olives is great for nibbling on. Source some good quality olives from a market or delicatessen as a wee treat. Remember a small bowl will suffice.

★ When the light levels improve try sprouting seeds – sprouts are a veritable smorgasbord of nutrients.

★ Try the following beetroot and carrot salad.

## Salad Sprinkle

★ Equal measures of sunflower and pumpkin seeds.

★ Toss the seeds into a heavy bottom saucepan on a medium / low heat. Keep the seeds moving until they brown.

★ Don't get distracted and do something else as they will burn, then you'll need to start all over again.

★ Cool in a bowl and store in a jar in the fridge for up to four weeks.

★ Brilliant for sprinkling on salads, adding to couscous, breakfast cereal, porridge, or even just to nibble on.

# Beetroot and Carrot Salad

2 medium carrots
2 medium fresh beetroot, peeled
Handful of salad sprinkle (see page 20), or use raw seeds
½ lemon, juiced
½ tbsp extra virgin olive oil

★ Easy! Grate the carrot, then the raw beetroot. Keep in separate bowls until serving to keep the carrots orange.
★ To serve, mix carrot and beetroot together, sprinkle with salad sprinkle (recipe below) and drizzle the olive oil and lemon juice on top.
★ If you have leftovers, simply add more freshly grated carrot to renew the spectacular colour combination. The natural bright colours of the beetroot and carrot indicate that it's packed with antioxidants.

# Couscous with Steamed Veggies

*Serves four, or two for dinner and two packed lunches*

Couscous is the chieftain of instant meals. Just add boiling water. Don't bother buying the pre-packaged flavoured stuff. Making couscous from scratch is much cheaper and better for you and requires hardly any effort. Leftover couscous keeps well in the fridge for a couple of days and makes a tasty leftover lunch. This recipe makes enough couscous for four servings, so for two, reserve half of the cooked couscous and take for lunch the next day.

  300g couscous
  550ml boiling water
  1 tsp butter / olive oil
  ½ vegetable stock cube
  Sea salt or herbamere (organic herb salt) to taste

A selection of veggies for steaming, pick a variety of colours for maximum nutritional variation: carrot, sweet potato, butternut squash, pepper, sweetcorn, cauliflower, broccoli, courgette, mushroom, spinach, herbs for flavour.

★ Whilst you're steaming the vegetables, place the couscous and half a crumbled stock cube in a microwave safe container or saucepan with a lid.

★ Boil 550ml of water and add it to the couscous.

★ Stir through and microwave on high for 30 seconds. Alternatively, cook on the hob on a very low heat for 5 minutes.

★ Add a teaspoon of butter and fork through couscous to separate the grains. You can also add some freshly chopped parsley, chives, coriander, basil or dill for extra flavour. Let it sit for a couple of minutes whilst you're finishing steaming your vegetables.

★ If microwaving, cook the couscous for a further 30 seconds, then heap onto two plates.

★ Serve the steamed vegetables on top of the couscous.

## For Lunch

Into the leftover plain couscous stir through a mixture of your favourite antipasto: olives, sundried tomato, freshly chopped herbs, chopped artichoke hearts, rocket, fresh chopped tomato, grilled mushrooms, roast red pepper, and harissa or pesto to taste. Voila! Couscous salad.

# HOT! HOT! HOT! Baked Potatoes

Yes, the humble spud is a tasty and cheap standby for when you're really not in the mood (to cook). Eaten with the skin on, they provide nearly half of your daily vitamin C and are a good source of potassium and fibre. One medium-sized potato has 100 calories and provides complex carbohydrates needed to fuel our brains and bodies. Baked potatoes have bad press as they are high GI (quick burning carbs), but personally I find them an easy nutritious meal.

To bake a potato, scrub well then prick the skin all over with a fork and bake in an oven at 220°C for an hour and a quarter. If you're in a hurry, microwave for a few minutes and finish off in a pre-heated oven. Cut a cross in the top and mash the middle with a fork.

The trick is to keep the toppings healthy, so here are some ideas:

★ Fresh rocket with a splash of balsamic vinegar is a flavoursome green option. Rocket stands up to the heat of a potato better than lettuce, which tends to go limp.

★ Garlic mushrooms: Melt a tablespoon of butter in a non-stick frying pan on a medium heat and add three (yes three) sliced cloves of garlic to a couple of handfuls of sliced mushrooms. Push around with a wooden spoon, adding a touch of water when the pan dries out to get a good garlic-ey brown sauce. Makes enough for two.

★ Baked beans (check the nutrition label for the healthiest brand, or make your own) with fresh thyme or parsley.

★ Vegetarian haggis is great on baked tatties, and really filling.

★ Fresh tomato with finely chopped onion and torn basil. Add a drizzle of olive oil, squeeze of lemon and a tiny bit of sugar if you are using 'inferior' tomatoes (i.e. any tomatoes purchased in Scotland at this time of year).

★ Instead of sour cream, try a dollop of houmous, cottage cheese or natural yoghurt on top. If you insist on melted cheddar cheese in your potato, use half of what you would usually use, grate it finely and mash it into the potato.

# Resisting Temptation Hints of the Month

## Eat Cake for Breakfast

Do you like chocolate? Most people eat sweet treats in the evening. If you'd like to enjoy a wee sweet something, have it early in the day. You're likely to burn it off as you are more active during the day. Any wee treats you snack on late at night, you might as well imagine patting onto your thighs and sleeping with. Nice.

## Be Selfish

If the only reason you buy biscuits and cakes is to cater for your other half, reconsider. It's worth having a chat about whether you really need tempting 'treats' in the house. Keep treats as treats, to be had every now and again. So you don't need to buy them with your everyday shopping.

## Drink More

It's an oldie but a goodie. It's easy to confuse thirst with hunger. Sometimes when we feel 'hungry' we're actually thirsty. So if you find yourself a bit peckish, try having a drink of water. I like the discipline of making myself a cup of herbal tea. By the time I've finished it, quite often I forget that the reason I made it was because I thought I was hungry. Works equally well if you find yourself getting the munchies in the evening – just make yourself a nice big pot of herbal / green tea.

# Fad or Fab

## Powerball

Powerball is a gyroscopic arm trainer. "What on earth is that?" I hear you ask. It's a plastic ball that fits in the palm of your hand. It has a gyro inside it (like a spinning top), that you set off spinning by pulling a cord. To keep it spinning, you need to move it in a circular motion with your wrist, forearm, and if you've really got it going, upper arm. The faster it spins, the more force it produces and consequently the more difficult it is to manipulate. Fascinating science experiment but is it any use?

We've got one in the house and whilst I can't get the thing to work, my significant other is more adept at it. It's meant to improve grip strength, good for racket sports and guitar playing. I have heard reports that it does indeed give a good arm workout, however the trick is to actually use the thing (like with many inspired fitness products on the market). Whilst it certainly looks fun – you can get glow in the dark versions – whether or not it gets used is another issue altogether. More a toy than a workout…

## Thigh Master

You may have one of the weird devices hidden in a cupboard somewhere. If not, don't bother rushing out and buying one. Advertised on TV infomercials in the eighties and nineties, the Thigh Master promised viewers lean thighs whilst watching the TV. My advice is to stop watching TV and get outside for a walk. Or try walking stairs up two at a time.

The Thigh Master is a padded device that is squeezed between the knees. You can get a similar benefit from squeezing a slightly flat rubber beach ball between your knees, offering resistance, or doing some inner thigh exercises without a device. It's another case of selling the public something that they definitely do not need… Utter piffle.

# Exercise of the Month: Happy Feet

Do you ever think about your feet? Have you ever considered what an amazing piece of design they are? How much they deal with each day? They deserve to be treated right. Feet, like any part of the body, can be exercised and it's a great way help avoid lower leg injuries. Try walking barefoot around the house, and clenching and relaxing your toes when sitting down.

If you exercise, it might be an idea to have a session with a podiatrist who can scrape and preen your feet to make them more comfortable. It's amazing how removing calluses can change the way you walk, and I highly recommend a foot MOT.

*Interesting fact: Podiatrist is the new term for chiropodist.*

# February Articles

## Carbohydrates: Friend or Foe?

Humans are omnivorous – we're designed to eat both plant and animal matter. Actually more than half of our diet comprises of plant matter (carbohydrates), so why are some diet fads so insistent on cutting them out?

To understand the rationale behind diets like the Atkins, you need to know a bit about carbohydrates. Carbohydrates (or carbs for short) are units of sugar joined together. The molecules vary in length from short (sweet fructose in fruit) to very long (non-digestible fibre). Carbs provide the necessary fuel (glucose) the body needs to operate.

Any fuel that is not used during the day is stored in the body for future use as glycogen (a form of glucose). This is a good thing – it is your energy reserve you need for when you're not eating. If too many carbs are eaten, over time, this may be stored as fat. The trick is to ensure that you are eating enough, but not too many carbs.

Another important point to consider is what kind of carbs you eat. There are carbs that burn quickly, causing a rapid peak in blood sugar (i.e. sweets, white bread, cornflakes), and there are slower burning carbs that cause a more controlled raise in blood sugar (i.e. porridge, pulses and nuts). It is the slower burning carbs that we should aim to consume.

It helps to have some understanding of the Glycaemic Index. In a nutshell, the GI (Glycaemic Index) is a measure of how fast your body turns food into fuel. On the index glucose is 100 as it burns quickly. The lower down the scale, the slower it burns. Hence lower GI foods leave you with a sense of feeling fuller for longer.

The low-down is that our bodies are specifically designed to use *mainly* carbohydrates, not proteins (from meat, cheese etc as prescribed by the Atkins), as an energy source. Proteins are used primarily to build tissue and repair our bodies. They're not as easily broken down into fuel (glucose).

This means that on restrictive diets like the Atkins, our bodies are not getting the nutrients we need, or the energy that we require. Whilst protein high, carb low diets may cause a temporary change in weight, they are not a long-term solution. A healthy body needs a balanced diet of both slow-burning carbs as well as protein.

# Raw Food Rules, OK?

Raw foodism, otherwise known as rawism, is gaining momentum as a backlash to all the processed junk around. More and more people are realising that raw food is a key to weight loss, increased energy levels and clear skin.

How much cooked food do you eat? Technology advances in the kitchen means that we cook, process and store our food for longer. Cooking may make meat edible, certain vegetables tastier and prolong shelf life, but what does it do to the molecular structure of your food?

Raw food contains enzymes that assist digestion, as well as nutrients to keep the immune system, and the body as a whole, in peak condition. Heating food to a high temperature destroys many of the important living enzymes in food. I remember someone explaining it to me years ago thus; if you think of a plant growing, there is a certain amount of energy in the plant (through photosynthesis etc). By picking the fruit, you effectively have some energy captured in the raw fruit. As the picked fruit gets older, it loses freshness, vitamins and energy. If cooked, the elevation in temperature changes its natural state; its texture and colour changes, and the molecular structure changes.

Here are some things to consider:

How natural is your food?

Has it been processed?

How was it grown?

How old is it?

If you keep your diet as unprocessed and untreated as possible, it's logical that you're going to feel healthier for it.

# Some Healthy Snacks

Healthy snacks are essential to maintain good energy levels and trim your waistline. A mid morning snack halfway between breakfast and lunch will keep your metabolism ticking over. You will also feel less hungry later in the day and be less prone to gorge on junk food.

My tip for healthy snacking is to prepare in advance. Spend 10 minutes in the evening sorting out your lunch bag and hang it off the back of your front door so you don't forget it in the morning. Fill it with fruit, wee sandwich bags of healthy nuts, seeds and dried fruit, oatcakes, and home made sandwiches.

Did you know that pre-packaged sandwiches contain up to 30g of fat per sandwich? Making your own in advance is not only cheaper, but also a lot healthier. If preparing the night before and you're worried about them going soggy, remember to put dry fillings next to the bread and other fillings in the middle. Alternatively, chop a lunchbox of salad and make your own sandwich in your work kitchen, or use bread rolls as they are less prone to sogginess. Remember to use wholegrain bread as it will keep you going for longer. Spend a bit extra and buying decent bread fresh from a baker. I like simple vegemite (or marmite) sandwiches on good quality fresh wholegrain bread, and yes, with only a scraping of butter. If you have good bread, you don't need loads of fat on it.

I am an enthusiastic advocate of oatcakes. They're a good slow burning snack that can be taken anywhere. Many brands are available in dinky packets, perfect for slipping into your work bag or desk drawer. Oats are a good source of vitamin E, zinc, selenium, copper, iron, manganese, magnesium and protein, and are also thought to help lower cholesterol.

Try to avoid buying pre chopped vegetables and salad from supermarkets. They are an overpriced way to buy veg and lose a lot of their goodness as the surfaces oxidise once chopped. A chopping board and a knife is all you need to make carrot sticks. If you need a salad on the run, try a local snack bar as the salad will be freshly chopped and not bagged in nitrogen as is the case of supermarkets.

**Some more ideas:**

★ Fresh fruit, you can chop it up to make it more appealing. Apples are a low GI snack as the pectin makes you feel fuller.

★ Pasta salad.

★ Carrot sticks and houmous.

★ Oatcakes, of course.

★ A bowl of cereal. Live life on the edge and try good quality muesli mixed with yoghurt.

★ Homemade popcorn (with a little salt or butter).

★ Mix of sunflower and pumpkin seeds.

★ Small handful of mixed raw nuts: unsalted almonds, cashews, brazil nuts

* Natural yoghurt with sliced banana and honey. Flavoured yoghurt sold in dinky pots can be kept in your work fridge.
* Wholegrain toast with pumpkin seed butter, available from health food shops.
* A hard boiled egg.

## Boost Your Immune System the Natural Way

Ever felt over winter that you can't be bothered exercising? Perhaps it's the weather, perhaps you feel a big sluggish, or maybe you just can't stand exercising in the dark.

Whatever your reason, it's heartening to remember that regular exercise can substantially boost your immune system in the long-term. Whilst you are exercising immune cells circulate through your body more quickly and therefore are better able to kill viruses and bacteria. If you imagine your rate of blood flow increasing as your heart rate goes up, it explains why the immune cells are able to 'cover more ground'. After exercise, this drops back to normal. Exercising also temporarily boosts the production of macrophages, the cells that attack bacteria. So, it's good all round.

An excellent article on the About.com website states,

"According to professor David Nieman, Dr. PH., of Appalachian State University, when moderate exercise is repeated on a near-daily basis there is a cumulative effect that leads to a long-term immune response. His research showed that those who walk at 70 – 75% of their VO2 Max for 40 minutes per day had half as many sick days due to colds or sore throats as those who don't exercise."

Quite often a client turns up who is feeling under the weather. We will generally do some gentle strength work to some groovy music and then finish with a really good stretch. I know that a gentle workout may actually help the individual feel better. My general rule of thumb about exercising when unwell is to do only what you feel able.

It is worth noting that intense cardiovascular exercise is not necessarily better than slower. This is because extended high intensity exercise can put the body under undue oxidative stress. If you are fighting an infection and then exercising super hard, you can put your body under undue stress, so it may not fight an infection so effectively. In fact, it can have the reverse effect and make you more vulnerable to illness. So listen to your body.

Of course good nutrition is crucial…And on a final note, remember that rest is as important as activity, so be sure to get a good night's sleep to keep your immune system in tip top shape.

## Food, but Not as We Know It

A few years ago I devoured Scottish food writer Joanna Blythman's excellent book *Shopped: The Shocking Power of British Supermarkets*. From Blythman I learnt all about how supermarket ready meals are basically a ploy by the big guys to 'value add' products and earn more dosh. That is, the more a food is processed, or pre-prepared for you, the greater the profit margin for the supermarket (and the less the nutrition for you). There's not much profit to be made from potatoes, but if you process them in some way, turn them into oven chips for example, you not only make more money, but as a side effect, much of the goodness and nutrition of the potato is removed. I'm not for one second implying that the primary aim of ready meals is to deny you valuable nutrients, but it is a side effect of having a machine mush up substandard ingredients into a ready meal.

As ready meals are mechanically processed, it means that the human body needs to do less processing to digest them. This means that processed foods tend to be higher on the Glycaemic Index, as the body doesn't need to do so much 'processing' of the food itself. Compare ready made soups to home made soups – which one to do you think will give you better nutrition and satisfy you more?

The more sophisticated our society gets, the more complicated our food gets... and further removed from actual 'food' it is. Our digestive systems haven't evolved in the last fifty years, but it is truly mind boggling how much our food has. We have seen a massive shift from producing food ourselves to multinational corporations manufacturing it for us. The emphasis has gone from eating what was nutritious and available locally, to buying foodstuffs that taste nice with the least amount of effort. It's also interesting to note the prevalence of modern (and largely Western) digestive health conditions that are also on the increase, such as IBS, gluten intolerance and food allergies in general. That's without getting into eating disorders such as bulimia and anorexia nervosa, or even touching on diabetes.

With all our labour saving devices, is it really true that we no longer have time to feed ourselves properly? Large producers certainly want us to think that. Breakfast cereals are a good example of one of the original ready meals, just add milk. Big business can make a much bigger profit by taking raw products (i.e. corn) and processing them, then adding back in chemically fortifying vitamins and minerals that have been processed from the raw state (i.e. corn flakes). Before cereal, most British households had a big cooked breakfast. With more women joining the workforce, and the advent of television advertising, breakfast cereals found their niche in the nations psyche. This is despite the fact that most cereals are as nutritious as the cardboard box they come in. The traditional Scots meal of porridge has become trendy again for good reason.

Another very interesting read is *The End of Overeating* by David A Kessler. If you have ever been at the mercy of a packet of digestive biscuits and scoffed the lot, this is the book for you. You are normal, the biscuits are freaky. Food producers have perfected the flavour balance that makes them remarkably enjoyable to eat, and therefore you buy more. Major food producers are aware of the irresistibility of the salt / fat / sugar combo. If there's any food you find yourself eating compulsively, it is likely that it's high in all salt / fat / sugar. Think of buttered toast (mmmmmm), which is basically fat on salt /sugar added bread. We have lost connection with what our body needs, namely nutrients, in sacrifice for foods that our brains tell us we like (salt / sugar / fat).

Michael Pollan's New York Times bestseller *The Omnivores Dilemma* sums it up nicely:

"Add fat or sugar to anything and it's going to taste better on the tongue of an animal that natural selection has hard wired to seek out energy-dense foods. Animal studies prove the point: Rats presented with solutions of pure sucrose or tubs of pure lard – goodies they seldom encounter in nature – will gorge themselves sick."

Pollan's book *In Defence of Food* has it in a nutshell with his 'Eater's Manifesto' "Eat food. Not too much. Mostly plants."

## Now onto the Economics, or... Put Your Money Where Your Mouth Is

Edinburgh is in the minority of British cities. We have a huge variety of independently owned local shops, and we need to remember to frequent them so they stay in business. My In-laws who live on the outskirts of Leeds no longer have a local shop, and their closest place to buy milk is a distant supermarket, a car drive away. They don't even have a choice of where to shop locally; lucky Edinburghers do.

Consider how many Tesco supermarkets there are nowadays. In Leith alone, we have had three Tescos open in the last two years. Supermarkets have the financial clout to change urban landscapes, whilst small local businesses are being put out of business by the sheer scale of these retail giants. If you talk to any of the convenience store owners, you'll discover that they're feeling the squeeze of the big guns. Supermarkets have massive power in their supply chain; suppliers are often asked to slash prices so supermarkets can run BOGOF (buy one get one free) deals and are subject to long waits to be paid for their wares. Processed food that has a high profit margin and long shelf life tend to be the only things that are better value at a supermarket. For affordable fresh fruit and vegetables, try a greengrocer.

Convenience is the main reason most people go to supermarkets, but at what price?

# MARCH

It's a month of good intentions, as the days promise to get warmer and summer holidays are on the horizon. It's also the start of British Summertime, so evenings are lighter for getting outdoors.

## WHAT'S IN SEASON

**Brussels sprouts, cabbage, cauliflower, celeriac, chicory, forced rhubarb, leeks, Jerusalem artichoke, kale, parsnip, purple sprouting broccoli, shallots, squash.**

## OATCAKE TOPPING OF THE MONTH

Banana mashed on oatcake makes a very satisfying snack. Turn it into an oaty banoffie pie by drizzling with honey.

# Easy Spring Recipes

## Soy Sunflower Seeds

Heat a dry pan to a low heat and toast a handful of sunflower seeds, stirring constantly. They will go brown and smell nutty. Take the pan off the heat and stir in a tiny splash of light soy sauce. The soy sauce will coat the seeds and dry out. They store well in the fridge (if you have any left) and make a moreish healthy snack.

## Tabbouleh

*Tabbouleh is the traditional salad served with felafel. Bulghur wheat is a common ingredient in Middle Eastern cuisine. It has a lower GI and higher nutritional content than couscous. In addition to tabouleh, bulghur wheat can also be used for stuffing or pilaf.*

*Serves four*

> 75g bulghur wheat
> 4 tomatoes, seeded and diced
> ½ cucumber, peeled and diced
> 4 spring onions, chopped
> Big handful parsley, finely chopped
> Small handful mint leaves, finely chopped
> ½ lemon, juiced
> 1 tbsp olive oil

★ Place the bulghur wheat in bowl and cover with 225ml boiling water. Soak for 30 minutes; drain and squeeze out excess water.

★ In a mixing bowl, combine the bulghur, tomatoes, cucumbers, onions, garlic, parsley, mint, lemon juice and olive oil. Toss and refrigerate for at least two hours before serving. Toss again prior to serving.

## The Easy Way to Cook Brown Rice

*A few years ago I discovered how good brown rice is. There are detox diets that revolve around brown rice – it's nutritious and easily digested by the body. It's wonderful stuff, but most people don't know how to prepare it. After you've got it started, you can leave it and forget about it. So simple.*

Either 1¾ cups rice to 3 cups of water (serves 4)

Or 2⅓ cups rice to 4 cups of water (serves 6)

★ Measure the uncooked rice into a sieve and wash thoroughly, picking out any funny looking bits.

★ Drain, then rinse again just to be sure. Drain again and shake off excess water

★ In a heavy bottomed big pot, heat a tablespoon of good quality oil. I like coconut oil.

★ Sauté the drained rice, stirring constantly until it smells nutty.

★ At the same time, boil the amount of water you need in a kettle.

★ After a minute or two of heating and stirring the rice, add the boiling water. Be careful, as it may spit.

★ Give it all a good stir and bring it to the boil.

★ Now move the pot to your smallest burner on the lowest flame.

★ Cook, covered with a tight lid for 45 minutes. Do not stir, and if it bubbles then it's too hot.

★ After 45 minutes turn the heat off and let it sit for another 15 minutes.

★ Serve with stir fry, or for one of the recipes below.

## Really Tasty Brown Rice

Allow rice to cool slightly, then add 1 small tin of sweetcorn kernels, 1 cup cooked edamame beans (shelled soy beans), a handful of pumpkin or sunflower seeds, a teaspoon of sesame seeds, a handful of your favourite chopped fresh herbs. Serve with a wedge of lime. You can divide the rice into various plastic containers and mix different vegetables and flavour combinations. If you've had a period of indulgence, it's good to give the system a break from strong flavours and heavy food. Have simple brown rice as two of your meals a day for a day or two and you'll be regular as clockwork.

## Healthy Fried Rice

Here's a healthy fried rice recipe, quick and easy for lunch or when you get home from work.

Using a non stick frying pan on a fairly high heat, melt a small amount of coconut oil and toss in some garlic / ginger / onion. The better your pan, the less fat you'll need to use, so it's worth investing in a good frying pan. Sauté briefly then add as much brown rice as you require, keep stirring. I like to throw in whatever I have handy, sliced mushrooms, cashews, tofu, sliced red pepper are some favourites. Crack one free range organic egg (per person) into the rice and keep stirring. The rice will start to smell nutty and the egg will cook quickly if you're stirring it well. Garnish with fresh coriander, parsley or whatever herbs you fancy.

What makes it healthy? The rice is brown, coconut oil is a healthy oil high in lauric acid, the eggs and nuts offer protein, with fresh herbs and vegetables for vitamins.

## Energy-Giving Pasta Salad

Pasta salad makes a great lunch – it's easy to prepare, full of goodness and keeps well out of a fridge (it actually tastes better when not fridge cold). Good for picnics and the great outdoors.

For two people, cook ½ packet of pasta (penne or bows, a short variety that's easy to eat with a fork only). I usually cook a whole packet for dinner and keep half aside to make pasta salad for the following day. When you've cooked and drained the pasta, toss it in a large salad bowl with a big dollop of pesto. This stops the pasta sticking together. Let it cool.

Now you can get inventive, add a selection of the following:

Sun dried tomatoes
Stoned olives
Capers
Finely chopped red onion
Oven roast or fresh peppers
Fresh herbs i.e. basil, parsley, oregano, chives
Rocket or shredded little gem lettuce (choose a lettuce with thicker leaver
that won't go soggy easily)
Chilli peppers
Spring onion
Chopped tomatoes
Small bits of gorgonzola / blue cheese
Chopped cucumber
Garlic, grilled or fresh mushrooms
Tinned sweetcorn
Roasted pine nuts
Drizzle balsamic vinegar
Sea salt and freshly ground pepper

That's it. Easy hey?

## Warm Roast Vegetable Salad

*Serves four, or two for dinner with leftovers for lunch (serve at room temperature, so no need to refrigerate it when you get into the office).*

1 – 2 beetroots
3 potatoes
2 sweet potatoes
½ butternut squash (optional)
Olive oil
Sea salt
3 – 6 garlic cloves
5 shallots or spring onions
1 cob corn, corn cut off or 3 tbsp tinned corn
1 red pepper
1 – 2 courgettes

Block of feta cheese
Handful olives
Packet of rocket

This recipe is a great time saver, as there are four simple steps each of 10 minutes, so you can 'cut as you go'. Be sure to keep a check on the roasting in between steps to prevent burning.

★ Start by preheating your oven to 200°C.

★ Then peel and chop the beetroot and potatoes into 1cm cubes.

★ Toss into a roasting tray and drizzle with olive oil and a little sprinkle of sea salt. Set your kitchen timer for 10 minutes and pop into the oven. You may wish to keep the beetroot segregated from the potato at this stage, as it will make the potato purple.

★ Over the next 10 minutes, peel and chop your sweet potato and butternut squash into similar sized cubes. If you don't have squash handy, you can simply add more sweet potatoes. When the kitchen timer goes, add them to the roasting tray, then set the timer for a further 10 minutes.

★ In the meantime, peel and cut garlic cloves into halves, red pepper into 1cm wide strips and courgette into batons. When the timer goes off, add them to the tray and give it a good toss. You may need to add a little extra olive oil at this point to prevent sticking.

★ Cook for another 10 minutes, keeping an eye on it and tossing when required. In this time, cube the feta, prepare the olives and rinse the rocket.

★ Remove tray from oven and let cool for 10 minutes.

★ Add the feta, olives and rocket and combine. Serve and eat immediately.

## Rhubarb! Rhubarb!

You can enjoy forced (grown in the dark) rhubarb from early February, bright pink and perfect in fruit crumbles on a chilly day. Forced rhubarb is replaced with field-grown rhubarb from April, which is less tender, but often more flavoursome. Rhubarb is popular in the UK mainly because it's such an easy vegetable to grow. Once established, the plant will last for years ('forcing' it will diminish its lifespan though). Rhubarb is a good source of fibre and contains moderate levels of vitamin C and calcium. Stewed rhubarb is perfect with natural yoghurt and muesli for breakfast; it also freezes well.

When growing up, one of the first recipes I learned from my Mum was fruit crumble, which I always believed was made with muesli. My version of rhubarb crumble is basically stewed fruit with hot muesli on top.

*For stewed rhubarb:*

Rhubarb, cut into inch long pieces
1 tbsp orange juice per stick
1 tsp brown sugar per stick

★ Put the rhubarb in a saucepan, add the OJ and sprinkle on a generous amount of sugar.
★ Cover with a close fitting lid and simmer on a very low heat until tender, about 5 minutes.

*For the crumble topping:*

Enough muesli to cover top of fruit, about an inch thick
Melted butter as required
Plain flour as required
Dark sugar and mixed spice to taste

★ It's unscientific I know, but when making crumble, I just toss the stewed fruit into a heat proof dish and then manually work out how much crumble topping I will need.
★ In a separate bowl, pour enough muesli to top the fruit and mix in enough melted butter to coat the muesli.
★ Add around 1 tbsp plain flour, some spice and sugar to taste and mix through. Top the fruit with this mixture.
★ Cook on 175°C until heated through and golden on top.

A quick and easy alternative for a chilly day is to spoon some stewed fruit into a bowl, top with muesli and microwave or cook in an oven until warm. Rhubarb also works well stewed with apple.

*Here's an interesting fact for culture vultures: The word rhubarb is often used by actors talking quietly to one another onstage to simulate real conversation, since it contains no harsh sounding consonants and is hard to detect… "rhubarb, rhubarb, rhubarb"*

# Resisting Temptation Hints of the Month

## Have Healthy Food Ready

It's good to have a hearty lunch. As the old saying goes, breakfast like a king, lunch like a prince and dinner like a pauper… or something like that. Prepare your morning food in advance, so it's easy for you the next day. Measure oats and water into a bowl / saucepan for porridge to soak overnight, so all you need to do in the morning is cook the porridge in its container.

Use time when preparing your evening meal to pack a lovely morning snack to take to work. Into the lunch bag go oatcakes, fruit, a small bag of assorted nuts and dried fruits and maybe even a wee square of dark chocolate as a treat. Make double quantities of your dinner (especially if it's soup, pasta or anything reheatable) and save half for lunch the next day.

By planning your food for the next day, you make it easier to fuel yourself adequately… even if you're distracted by that pesky work nonsense.

## Get Fruity

Buy yourself a nice fruit bowl and make it a centrepiece of your kitchen table. Each weekend, fill it with your favourite fruit and every morning grab a few pieces to take to work. Buy a variety of fruit, including avocados (which need usually need home ripening anyway), and make sure that the fruit bowl is your first stop in the kitchen for a snack. Seedless grapes are a low calorie snack if you feel like picking on something in the evening. If you find some of your fruit over ripening, use it in a smoothie.

## A Chocolate Challenge

Do you consider yourself a chocoholic? If so, what kind of choccy do you nibble on? Is it Dairy Milk or is it dark 85% chocolate? If it's the latter, then you can officially consider yourself a chocoholic, but that's not necessarily a bad thing.

Dark chocolate in moderation (i.e. one or two squares) can have health benefits. It contains flavenoids that are thought to help lower blood pressure and also antioxidants which help fight free radicals. So next time you crave something sweet, ditch the Dairy Milk and go for a square or two of the darkest chocolate you can find and discover 'proper' chocolate.

# Fad or Fab

## Dumbbells

Dumbbells are what I refer to as 'old school' kit. They're usually held one in each hand as various exercises are undertaken. The advantage of dumbbells over weights machines is that you control the movement as you lift, so stabilising muscles are engaged. They are also good for co-ordination and developing even strength through both sides. With machine weights and even barbells (a long bar with weights on each end), it's easiest to favour the dominant side so your non-dominant side has an easy ride. Not so with dumbbells.

The disadvantage of dumbbells is (obviously) that they are heavy to move around, but they do make a good door stop should you require it. JJB Sports and Argos have a selection of dumbbells of a good weight (the 'baby' weights under 2kg won't do much for you unless you do loads of reps). You won't bulk up from doing dumbbells alone, but you might find yourself the proud owner of a toned upper body.

To quote Wikipedia: "Dumbbells as a word originated in Tudor England – athletes used hand-held church bells to develop the upper body and arms. These bells ranged in weight from a few ounces to many pounds. The bells were flourished in various ways. This would have made a great deal of noise, so the athletes would take out the clappers so they could practice quietly; hence the name "dumb", as in "no sound", and "bell" – dumbbell. When strongmen started to make their own equipment they kept the name even though the shape changed. The etymology of the word "kettlebell" is similar."

## Sweat Suits

Otherwise known as sauna suits, these vinyl or plastic suits are meant to encourage sweating whilst you work out. Ick. The websites that sell these overpriced plastic suits promise that the thermogenic effect (i.e. temperature raising) effect will boost your metabolism. Sadly for anyone who has bought one, this is not true.

Sweat suits make you lose sweat, yes, this is true. So the weight you lose is actually water and salts (i.e. you become dehydrated). Not an ideal state to be in when you exercise. The most common use for these is in amateur boxing where a boxer may try to make a lighter weight category. But even in these instances they are not recommended, as the boxer starts the fight dehydrated and is therefore disadvantaged. Looks like a bin liner, belongs in a bin.

## Exercise of the Month: Go Natural

If you usually pound the pavement, take the time this weekend to go for a meander on grass or bare earth. You will feel well-grounded and it will give your knees, ankles and feet a break from unforgiving concrete.

# March Articles

## Exercise in the Great Outdoors

As the days get longer and the weather warmer, it's a good time to start exercising outdoors. Fair weather cyclists and runners have started to appear on the streets, but what else is there to do outdoors? Following is a typical park workout that I would do on a sunny day.

**Warm up**: Jog around the park. Choose a good sized park, so an easy jog or fast walk around the perimeter is a good warm up, raising heart rate and core body temperature. Wear a heart rate monitor to make your cardio exercise measurable and to ensure your heart rate remains in the 'training zone' for the entire workout.

**Dynamic stretching**: Dynamic stretching is warming up a joint by taking it through its range of motion. Shoulder circles and shrugs warm up the upper body, combined with some gentle torso twisting. You can combine this with some dynamic leg stretches (kicking your rear with your heels, walking on the spot with knees high) to prepare for strength work.

**Strength exercises**: A park bench makes a fine foundation for many strength exercises. It's easy to learn how to do press ups on the back of a bench, tricep dips on the front, and using a resistance band looped through the bench. Learning new exercises is best from a qualified instructor, as they can correct your form and posture.

Grassy areas are perfect for lunges and squats, which you will find more challenging outdoors as your have to balance on uneven terrain. Grassy areas are also perfect for plyometrics (to put it simply, jumping type of exercises) as they absorb the shock more than tarmac.

**Interval training**: Interval training is basically where you go faster for some bits, and then let your heart rate recover before pushing yourself again. This can have a strict structure or you can utilise Fartlek training where you use natural landmarks such as trees and light poles as distance markers (i.e. sprint to one lamp pole, then recover for one, then sprint again etc). Alternatively if you have never run before, you can build up by jogging one lamp pole, walking the next and then jogging again. You can build up good distance this way and eventually run the whole way.

**Cardiovascular:** Outdoor space means you can push yourself, so set up some markers for sprint drills, using low walls for stepping and hills for getting your heart rate up: these are ways of using your everyday outdoor environment to add interest to your workout. Skipping rope and hula hooping are also fun cardio exercises.

**Cool down:** Use a park bench or wall to intensify calf stretches. If you are bendy enough, you can get your foot on the back of a park bench to stretch inner thigh and hamstrings. Alternatively walk or jog back home and enjoy a well-deserved stretch (and abs session if you wish) from the comfort of your lounge room.

## Your Range of Motion: Use it or Lose It

Have you ever experienced the feeling of 'stiffening up' when you have been sitting still for an extended time? Range of Motion (ROM) is a measurement of how flexible each joint is (the range that the joint can move in). It's a common term used by weightlifters, physiotherapists and other such folk, but it plays an important part in your everyday life.

Some people believe that exercising is only for those wanting to lose weight. Not so! Taking your body through a whole range of movement everyday is crucial for keeping joint flexibility and ease of movement generally. Some of the signs of ageing, for example stooping, can be addressed with regular exercise.

In modern times we are largely sedentary. Stop and think about your day for a minute. How much time do you spend sitting down, or standing still (for those in retail)? As humans have evolved we have got very good at doing things with the least amount of effort possible. In other words our intelligence and the evolution of technology have made it possible to exist with very little physical exertion. Gone are the days of scrubbing, washing by hand, beating rugs, walking to the grocery store and lugging heavy bags. Work nowadays tends to be more cerebral and less physical, which is why we need to take time out to take our bodies through a range of movements. By moving a joint through all the directions possible, you ensure that the joint has the sufficient length of tendons and ligaments (the bits that hold your joints together) to cope with all movements necessary.

Try this experiment – sitting on a chair, lift one leg slightly and draw a circle with the tip of your foot. Your knee and shin should stay still and the only your foot should move in a circle. Notice, is the 'circle' really circular? How much ROM do you have in your ankle? Practising every day will ensure that your ankles stay flexible, and able to deal with slips and trips.

By exercising regularly, not only will you feel more flexible and limber, but also less prone to injury, which is good news for every body.

## A Spring in Your Step

Newton's third law: "for every action, there is an equal and opposite reaction". Bet you never think of physics when you are out and about, but perhaps you should.

Newton's third law basically says that the harder you step, the more the reverberation. Have you ever wondered why you have sore legs after a long run (or even a hard day's shopping)? It's partly the shockwaves sent back up your legs from pounding the pavement.

Concrete is not a forgiving surface, nor is tarmac, or most other hard-wearing traffic-bearing materials. They're made like that to last. Do you think our forefathers and mothers would have sprinted across lengthy rock surfaces? Probably not. Our bodies are designed to step on softer surfaces, which is why so many long-distance roadrunners end up with shot knees, shattered tibias and shin splints.

Grass and dirt tracks absorb the shock from your legs more, and are spongier surfaces on which to run. Another interesting thing about off road running and walking is that the surface is likely to be more uneven, so you will need to concentrate more on where you put your feet. The advantage of this is that is will help strengthen your ankles and lower legs. However do be aware of twisted ankles, especially on pebbly or rocky tracks.

Running or walking on the beach is another idea. The deeper the sand, the more intense the workout. For a faster run or walk, stick close to the water on the hard sand. Masai Barefoot Technology shoes replicate the uneven feeling of walking on sand (based on the Masai tribe, who run great distances in the African sand). They're about £140 and are shaped like platform shoes with a curved sole. MBTs are meant to get the core muscles working through being inherently unstable. However, why pay top dollar for some shoes when you can walk on bare earth or sand yourself?

So consider changing your regular route to incorporate varying surfaces and feel the difference in your weary pegs. Viva la difference.

# Water, The Elixir of Life

Hydration is a much under-discussed topic. It's not as if we're stranded in the desert with only a cantankerous camel for company, an empty water bottle and sand as far as the eye can see. There's water everywhere, why should we have to think about drinking the stuff?

Guyton's *Textbook of Medical Physiology* states that "the total amount of water in a man of average weight (70 kilograms) is approximately 40 litres, averaging 57 percent of his total body weight. In a newborn infant, this may be as high as 75 percent of the body weight, but it progressively decreases from birth to old age, most of the decrease occurring during the first 10 years of life. Also, obesity decreases the percentage of water in the body, sometimes to as low as 45 percent".

We use water for everything from cushioning the body, to dissolving substances to circulate around the body, to removing toxins, keeping skin in good condition, and even lubricating eyeballs. It is not uncommon for people to get by not drinking water, or maybe only a glass or two a day. I know some people just don't get thirsty.

I have a theory about not-feeling-thirsty and it goes like this: many moons ago when we were hunter-gatherers, we did not always have access to water (or

24 hour supermarkets for that matter) and could only drink water when it was available. So when water was plentiful, we drank lots of it and were healthy. When water was scarce, the body stopped 'feeling' thirsty as a survival mechanism. If you don't drink much water, then you don't get thirsty in the same way that someone who drinks a lot of water does. So it's just a matter of getting into the habit of drinking more water, then you will get more thirsty, so it will become automatic. Presto! An easy way to become healthier. Just look at someone's skin and you can tell if they drink enough water or not.

Water also assists the body in its metabolic processes. So drinking more water can help you burn calories more easily as it assists the actual process of burning calories. Nifty, eh? For this reason, it is best to sip water throughout the day, rather than gulp a large amount at a time.

Whilst the weather is cold outside, the temperature is often overly warm and dry inside (not so much a problem in drafty tenement flats, but in modern housing, offices and buses where the temperature can be more tropical). Central heating dries out the skin, so in addition to using a good moisturiser, drinking loads of water will keep your complexion glowing. If cold water really isn't your thing, try keeping a filter jug at room temperature, or even hot water (you can add lemon and honey too). Since we're on the subject, my rule of thumb as to whether a drink counts as water is that it has to be non-caffeinated (as caffeine is a diuretic that flushes water out of your system), not a fizzy drink with artificial sweeteners and mainly comprising of… you guessed it, water.

Easy ways to help you drink more water:

★ Have a glass of water beside the bed.
★ Drink a glass of water upon waking as your body will be dehydrated from sleeping. If you have a morning coffee, have it after your glass of water.
★ Keep a bottle of water at your desk, and try to drink one bottle before lunch and one after.
★ For those on the go, carry a bottle of water with you. And remember to drink it, as it means your load will get lighter…
★ If you drink tea or coffee during the day, alternate with glasses of water.
★ Likewise, if you are indulging in some ethanol in the evening, rehydrate by alternating water with booze.

★ Use a filter jug and buy filters in bulk. Get a nice water bottle that can be washed or put in the dishwasher and fill it from the filter jug to carry around with you. Portable water without the waste.

★ If you run or power walk get a donut shaped water bottle that is easy to carry.

Salute, cheers and slainte… I'll drink (water) to that.

# APRIL

Spring is sprung, the grass is riz,
I wonder where the birdies is?
They say the bird is on the wing.
Isn't that absurd?
I always thought the wing was on the bird.

## WHAT'S IN SEASON

**Asparagus, broccoli, beetroot, carrots, cauliflower, leeks, mint, parsley, purple sprouting broccoli, radishes, rhubarb, spring onions.**

## OATCAKE TOPPING OF THE MONTH

Kidney Bean Pate: Take one can of drained kidney beans and combine with a selection from the cupboard: cumin, chilli sauce, pepper, squeezed lemon, a chopped spring onion and a handful of parsley. You can vary the ingredients to what you have available. Throw the whole lot in a blender and blend until creamy. Makes enough for about 20 oatcakes, keeps in the fridge for up to five days and is best served at room temperature.

# Easy Spring Recipes

## Lovely Mint

I like buying big bunches of mint from one of the many Asian supermarkets locally. Store mint in a jar of water in your fridge with the water level topped up. It's lovely for making fresh mint tea. Simply wash a few springs and pop them into a teapot with boiling water, you can also add a green tea bag. Serve with a couple of mint leaves in a heat-resistant glass.

Mint ice cubes are a great way to use up leftovers. Nip the top small leaves off each mint sprig and place them in an ice cube tray, top with water and freeze. For the larger leaves, rinse and chop finely, put into ice cube trays and top with water and freeze. These are fabulous for making mint tea, adding to smoothies or as a decoration for cool drinks.

## Buttery Beany Carrot Soup

*This recipe is so easy and tasty… Butter beans are low-fat, high protein, brimming with essential minerals and give the soup a lovely creamy texture.*

*Serves four starters, or two hungry people for mains.*

Dash olive oil
Tiny bit of butter (optional)
1 large onion, chopped
Medium tin (about 250g) of butter beans, rinsed
500g carrot, washed and chopped into chunks (you can leave the skin on)
750ml vegetable stock
Sprig fresh rosemary, chopped

★ Heat the olive oil (and optional butter) in a large pan and sauté the onion, keeping the lid on.
★ Add the carrot chunks and cook a bit longer to coat the carrots. Pop in some chopped rosemary.
★ Squeeze the butter beans out of their skins and add to the pot. Discard skins.
★ Give it a stir, then add the stock.
★ Cook for 20 to 30 minutes until carrots are tender. Season to taste.
★ Cool, then blend and reheat.
★ Voila! Very tasty!

Use a bit of butter at the beginning to bring out the buttery-ness of the beans. Only a tiny amount is needed and you can skip it if you are slimming. You can also use dried butter beans, but soak them overnight first, and cook the soup for 1 to 2 hours before blending.

## Warm Feta Salad

*Really simple and looks impressive too… Whilst the fat content in feta is about 20%, by combining it with salad and pita bread, it spreads the fat content out over the whole dish.*

*Serves two*

200g block feta cheese
Sprig fresh mint, chopped
Fresh thyme, parsley, oregano or other green herbs
1 whole red chilli (optional)
1 lemon, cut from it two circular slices, then juice the rest
Ground black pepper (no salt as feta is already salty)
Your favourite salad ingredients
2 wholemeal pita bread

- ★ Preheat oven to 200°C.
- ★ On a piece of tin foil, arrange half of the chopped herbs and chilli, a grind of pepper and a slice of lemon.
- ★ Place the block of feta on top of the herbs, then arrange the other half of the ingredients on top of the feta.
- ★ Wrap feta in foil into a parcel and place in the middle shelf of the oven.
- ★ Whilst this is under way, wash and arrange some lettuce and /or rocket leaves on two plates as the bed for the salads.
- ★ Sprinkle chopped olives, sun dried tomatoes, artichoke hearts, sliced red or green peppers, finely sliced mushrooms, red onion or whatever you fancy on and around the lettuce.
- ★ Drizzle with lemon juice and a touch of good quality olive oil.
- ★ After fifteen minutes, unwrap top of feta and move it down a shelf in your oven. Grill the pita bread in the top of the oven.
- ★ When the pita bread are warmed on both sides, slice each into six triangles and arrange around the plate of salad.
- ★ Remove feta from oven, chop in half and place in centre of the salad bed. Finish with another grind of pepper and enjoy.

*This is also a cracking recipe to take camping. Prepare the feta parcel in advance and keep it in a cool bag (an esky if you're Australian). You can cook it directly on hot coals, in a campfire, or on a BBQ.*

## Edamame Salad

You may have come across edamame (soya) beans in their pods at a Japanese restaurant. If you're a fan you'll be pleased to note that Chinese supermarkets, and increasingly, conventional supermarkets, stock frozen edamame beans.

Soya beans are great as they contain a whopping 14g protein per 100g and only 3.8g fat. They're truly a hero low fat high protein food, and also really versatile. You can simply boil them and serve as a side dish, but here is an exciting salad that tastes even better the day after you've made it:

500g edamame, fresh or frozen, cooked until tender
1 carrot, grated
1 shallot, minced

*Dressing*
50ml rice wine vinegar*
2 tbsp olive oil
2 tbsp coriander, chopped
1 tbsp light soy sauce
1 tbsp honey
1 tsp lemon juice

* from a Chinese grocers or in the Chinese section of the supermarket

★ Combine the cooked and cooled edamame with the carrot and shallot in a bowl
★ Whisk together the dressing ingredients and pour over the salad.
★ Toss well and refrigerate for at least two hours.

## Tempeh with Mushrooms

A little-known soy bean cousin of tofu, tempeh is rich in protein, calcium and iron. It tastes kind of nutty, and is used in Indonesian and Malaysian (and Australian) dishes. You can buy it fresh or frozen at good health food stores.

*Serves 2*

1 block (224g) tempeh, defrosted
8 – 10 mushrooms, try combining different varieties, roughly sliced
1 tbsp coconut or olive oil
Light soy sauce, to taste
2 cloves garlic, finely chopped
2 spring onions, chopped
Small handful of freshly chopped parsley or coriander
¼ courgette
½ carrot sliced (optional)
Handful of rocket to garnish

★ Slice block of tempeh down the middle to make two big blocks, then in half the other way, to make four slices. Chop these into stick shapes.
★ Sauté tempeh with oil in a non-stick frying pan, add vegetables, garlic, splash of soy sauce and water if it starts to stick.
★ Cook at a medium temperature, you can cover it for a bit to make sure the vegetables cook. Add the herbs near the end.
★ Serve with handfuls of fresh rocket and a slice of rye bread.

## 'The Best' Broccoli

*Broccoli can be considered a 'superfood' as it is dense in goodness – lots of antioxidants including vitamin C and folate (a B vitamin which may help heart disease).*

*Serves two over noodles as a main course, or four as a side dish.*

   1 medium broccoli
   ½ tbsp fresh grated ginger
   2 tbsp coconut or olive oil
   2 tbsp soy sauce
   2 tbsp red wine vinegar
   1 small dried chilli

★ Cut the broccoli into florets. You can include the broccoli stalk if you cut off the tough outer layer.

★ Heat the oil in a pan and sauté the ginger for a few seconds. Add the broccoli and stir fry on a high heat.

★ In a cup, mix the soy sauce and red wine vinegar and add a finely chopped chilli.

★ Pour the mixture over the broccoli and stir well. Reduce the heat to medium and cover the pan with a lid. Cook until just tender but still slightly crunchy.

Serves two over noodles as a main course, or four as a side dish.

# Resisting Temptation Hints of the Month

## Put a Lid on It

Keep a jar of almonds, seeds and dried fruit at the front of your cupboard, so it's the first thing you see when you have the munchies. Don't eat straight from the jar (as you may end up eating the lot), but pour a small handful into a tiny wee bowl and nibble.

## Easter Eggs

You don't need to deny yourself or your loved ones the joy of Easter eggs, instead opt for quality rather than quantity. There's an increasing range of dark chocolate, hand-made and organic Easter treats available nowadays, on the pricier side, but definitely better quality. You'll eat less of them and enjoy them more.

## Try a Different Grain

Do you like sandwiches? Toast? What kind of bread do you eat? 95% of the bread that you find in supermarkets is rubbish, with added chemicals to keep it from going mouldy. It's fun to splash out and try different breads. Rye bread from an independent bakery is likely to be more filling, less processed and better for you. Support your local baker and try their speciality loaf. My rule of thumb is that the heavier the bread, the better it is.

## Smaller Meals

Many of us eat large evening meals. To boost your metabolism, your dinner should be a small meal and your breakfast and lunch more substantial. Try serving less for dinner, perhaps on a smaller plate. You can always have seconds if you're still hungry, but remember to wait for half an hour (how long it takes for your dinner to go down) before replenishing your plate.

# Fad or Fab

## Heart Rate Monitors

A Heart Rate Monitor (HRM) consists of two pieces, a chest strap that electronically picks up your heart beat, and a watch-like monitor to which your heart rate is transmitted. Growing rapidly in popularity (and also dropping in price) this is an invaluable piece of kit for anyone training outwith a gym. Heart Rate training means that you train to your own fitness level, and will help you get fitter faster. I generally recommend an entry-level Polar brand monitor (about £40) as I find them reliable and foolproof. Fab.

## Flexi-Bar, the Wobbly Stick

Vibration training is big business, and the Flexi-bar falls firmly into this camp. The Flexi-bar is a big wobbly stick. You hold on to the middle and give it a shake. It's got weights at either end, so it wobbles as you work out and you work against the wobble. According to their website at www.flexi-bar.co.uk, "As you swing Flexi-bar, a vibration passes through your body. This vibration pushes and pulls the muscles out of equilibrium, a process known as the Tonic Stretch Reflex. During a Tonic Reflex Contraction signals are passed continuously from the muscles to the brain and back again, via the nervous system. These signals tell the muscles they are being pushed away from their centre and they must automatically contract to bring themselves back." In a similar sense to a PowerPlate, muscles contract against vibration.

I had a bash on a 'wobbly stick' when these first came out a few years ago (in a blaze of publicity). Yes, I did use muscular strength to hold on, but no, I don't think it's going to catch on.

## Gripads

Lifting weights is a fun pastime that can define your muscles and make you stronger. Putting on some groovy tunes and doing a good weights workout always gives me a bit of a buzz… except for the manly callouses that I develop on my hands. I was getting trademans' hands, so would sometimes wear cycling gloves. That is, until Gripads came and changed my life. As the website www.gripad.co.uk says, "they do what it says on the tin", i.e. they're a pair of protective pads for gripping weights. Definitely a fabulous innovation, if only because they're so obvious that I can't believe it's not been done before.

## Exercise of the Month: Go Batty

At the moment the evenings are light but still a bit too chilly to be sitting around. So if you like to make the most of your evenings after work, get down to your local park with a friend and a bat and ball. Any old bat (cricket, tennis) will do, and an old tennis ball is perfect. It doesn't matter if you're not a sporting superstar, just swat the bat around and hope for the best. It's amazing how much extra exercise you get when running after a ball hit in completely the wrong direction…

# April Articles

## Make a Splash With Aqua Aerobics

What do you imagine when you think of aqua aerobics? Many of us would imagine a jolly group of ladies bobbing about in a swimming pool. If you are a cinema buff, you may be reminded of Japanese ladies in the hotel pool in Sofia Coppola's *Lost in Translation*, possibly the only celluloid aqua aerobics moment in history.

A good aqua class can be an excellent low impact workout and will combine elements of heart raising activity (cardio) with strength work. This is the clever bit, as the resistance equipment used in the pool are floats (rather than weights). You may not think that pushing a foam dumbbell through the water would be difficult, but try it and you'll be surprised. It's a good way to develop lean and strong muscles, and you're less likely to injure yourself than in weight training. This cushioning effect of the water is what makes the workout effective, as it's working against the resistance of the water, making the simplest exercises as intense as you want. Aqua aerobics is highly recommended for pregnant women, less able bodies, older folks and anyone who likes to have a splash about.

Another good thing about exercising in water is that you keep cool and no one can see what you're doing with your legs – a boon if you consider yourself uncoordinated.

## Walking! How Pedestrian...

Walking, the natural form of propulsion for us as a species, is one of the best forms of exercise. Walking at a decent pace gives your lungs and heart a workout. It can burn calories very effectively and tone your body. Thirdly and by no means lastly, it's an environmentally friendly form of transportation.

Have you ever been bedridden from illness or unable to walk because of injury? You will know how frustrating it is to not be able to do one of the things we as humans take for granted. Going for a walk is a guaranteed way to beat any blues and give you a fresh perspective on life. Most of us walk at a pace that we feel comfortable at, with minimum exertion. As intelligent human beings, we like to get around at minimum effort. In the times of our great-grandparents we'd do lots of physical activity as part of our everyday life, so we needed to conserve energy when we could.

Times have changed. Nowadays we need to burn as much energy as we can when we exercise as the rest of our lives are so sedentary. To walk at a pace where you experience fitness benefits and 'fat burning' (i.e. using more body fat as fuel), you need to walk at a pace where you feel slightly breathless and 'puffed'. Some of us aren't used to pushing ourselves and can feel flushed and sweaty. Moving at this pace continuously for at least 30 minutes at least three times per week can offer significant fitness benefits. For some of us, it's simply speeding up our walk to work. For others, it may mean getting out and about more. Go on, get outdoors and see more of your surroundings on foot.

## Cycling, not just for kids

In an age of cost cutting and thinking green, cycling is officially cool. It's also the quickest way to get around cities. Cycling avoids dreaded road works and traffic jams, is free (once you've got a bike), is carbon neutral and as an added bonus, gives you nice legs.

Commuting to work by bike is an easy way to enjoy some pulse-raising cardio exercise every day. If you're worried about getting hot and flustered, remember that the more you ride, the easier it gets. If healthy glowing cheeks isn't your look, spend a couple of minutes when you arrive at your destination catching your breath.

According to www.bikebelles.org.uk, "Regular cyclists tend to have the fitness levels of someone 10 years their junior. Moderate pedal pushing burns up to 500 calories per hour, which is more than walking or swimming."

OK, so I've convinced you to jump on a bike, here are some things to be aware of:

★ Visibility in the evenings is often low, so invest in a high viz jacket or waistcoat. It makes all the difference and cars give you noticeably more room. Fluoro is bound to come back into fashion soon… Or just consider yourself a leftover from the rave scene.

★ Buy a Spokes map of Edinburgh to discover hidden cycle paths – at www.spokes.org.uk or from your local bike shop.

★ Use your manners and your bell on cycle paths. Pedestrians will not hear you approach from behind, and a 'thank you' when passing is always appreciated.

★ If your bike is coming out from winter hibernation, get it serviced. Working brakes can make the difference between stopping and a smash.

★ Enjoy your new found freedom.

## Get Fit and Enjoy It

Getting fit and staying in shape is a long-term proposition. Once you get to the shape you'd like to be, you need to sustain your fitness by exercising regularly. Quite often weight loss is the motivation to start exercising and it's easy to get fired up at this early stage. However keeping in shape means exercising regularly for the rest of your life.

The key is to find something that you enjoy doing. There are a few ways to do this. What kinds of activities did you enjoy as a child? Did you play football with your mates? Cycle to school? Go for long weekend meanders? Skip rope? Make up dance routines? If you were a sedentary youngster, perhaps now is the time to start considering something you've always wanted to do. The warmer months are the season of loads of charity challenges. If you're seriously deconditioned (i.e. out of shape), perhaps plan for a future event. Ever want to trek the Himalayas? There's lots of ways you can do it for charity. Having folk sponsor you is a very powerful motivator. I'm wondering if Eddie Izzard would have ever completed his extraordinary back to back marathons if he didn't have a camera crew following him. Find a way where you can't wriggle out of a commitment, and then (this is the important bit), be sure to prepare for it. Rope in a mate and chart your progress.

It's never too late to learn a new skill and the fitter you get, the easier it becomes and the closer you get to your goal. And the looser your clothes get. Nice. Also by enjoying regular exercise you are more likely to stick to it and see results.

# MAY

May is a month of lengthening days, blossom on the trees and slightly squiffy weather.

## WHAT'S IN SEASON

**Asparagus, beetroot, broccoli, carrots, garlic, leeks, lettuce and salad leaves, jersey royal potatoes, mint, parsley, purple sprouting broccoli, radishes, rhubarb, rocket, samphire, sorrel, spinach, spring onions, wild nettles.**

The long days are also a good time to start growing sprouts in your kitchen window. Alfalfa, mung beans and chick peas all make lovely and nutritious sprouts and are great for salads, stir fries and sandwiches.

## OATCAKE TOPPING OF THE MONTH

Oatcakes and homemade houmous go hand in hand flavourwise, and make a filling snack. You can enjoy a whole week of snacking for under £2.

# Some Springtime Recipes

## A Scientific Exploration of Houmous

I have eaten houmous since I was a youngster and viewed it as a healthy option to fatty spreads. Imagine my surprise when I examined the nutritional content of supermarket houmous and discovered it was over 25% fat!

As a University student, my hippy housemates and I would make 2 litres of houmous at a time and freeze it for future use. I decided to hark back to my student days and make my own to check the fat content.

Tin of chickpeas

1 lemon, juiced

1 tbsp tahini (sesame seed paste, a Middle Eastern ingredient now commonly available)

1 tbsp olive oil

1 clove garlic, you can use roast garlic for a mellower flavour

Pulverise! Add extra water, rather than oil, to get it to the consistency that you like.

This recipe contains 31g of fat altogether, or 8.9g per 100 grams (about 9%). This is the real deal and tastes more like authentic houmous than supermarket houmous (supermarkets add extra fat to make it more palatable to our taste). Jamie Oliver's recipe has twice the tahini and olive oil as this recipe, but I personally think the extra fat is not necessary. When making my own, I always use good quality olive oil, however supermarket brands use rapeseed oil as it is cheaper. It will also have less fat if you cook the dried chickpeas from scratch, as a tin of chickpeas has 7g fat, whilst dried equivalent has about 3g. To use dried chickpeas, soak in cold water overnight, change the water and then boil for a very, very long time until tender. The kind of thing I made time for when I was a student.

## Asparagus Galore!

Did you know that asparagus is a member of the lily family and contains more folic acid than any other vegetable? Nor did I, but I do know three easy ways to enjoy it whilst it's still in season…

To prepare the stalks, rinse under water then bend them individually until they snap. This is the easiest way to work out where the woody bit ends and the yummy bit begins.

## Steaming

Place asparagus in a steamer and steam for only a couple of minutes until it's bright green. Serve with a squeeze of lemon and ground pepper.

## Pan Method

You need a heavy bottom non-stick frying pan for this one (or a BBQ). Cook the asparagus on a very hot pan with nothing in. It will get slightly charred and retain it's flavour. Serve with a drizzle of olive oil and sea salt.

# Oven-Roasted Asparagus with Sizzling Halloumi

*This recipe uses halloumi, a soft springy cheese made in Cyprus. It's medium fat (for a cheese, about 24%) and doesn't melt when heated, making it perfect to accompany grilled vegetables or warm salads. You can buy it vacuum-sealed from your local global grocer.*

*Serves two*

Bunch of asparagus
Handful of cherry tomatoes
1 tbsp olive oil
Sea salt and pepper
Sprigs of thyme
½ block halloumi, rinsed
¼ lemon, squeezed

*Dressing*
¼ lemon, squeezed
1 tsp olive oil
½ tbsp capers, chopped
½ tbsp parsley, chopped

★ Heat the oven to 180°C.
★ Place the tomatoes, a drizzle of olive oil, thyme, salt and pepper into a oven proof dish and bake for 15 minutes.
★ Prepare asparagus as above and chop into thirds.
★ Roll to coat them in the tomato juices, and roast for a further 10 to 15 minutes or until tender.
★ Cut the halloumi into 1cm slices.
★ Heat olive oil in a non-stick frying pan and, when hot, cook the halloumi slices until golden brown on both sides.
★ Serve roast asparagus and tomatoes with halloumi and dressing on top. Lovely served with a green salad and steamed new potatoes.

# Spinach and Feta Pie

Here's a good way to use up lots of spinach. This recipe contains about 24g fat, 15g protein per serving and if you leave most of the pastry on your plate and enjoy the filling, it cuts the fat down to 14.5g fat per serving.

*Makes four servings*

200g – 300g spinach, rinsed with any stringy stalks pulled out
1 tbsp olive oil
4 spring onions, chopped
150g feta cheese, cubed
4 free range organic eggs, beaten
Filo or puff pastry
Milk for brushing and sesame seeds for the top

★ Preheat your oven to 210°C, and grease a baking dish with a little butter.
★ In a large bowl, combine the lightly beaten eggs with the cheese and ground black pepper (salt not required as feta is salty).
★ Sauté the chopped spring onions in 1 tbsp olive oil, allow to cool then add to the egg mixture.
★ Wilt the spinach in the previously-used pan. All you need to do is put the rinsed spinach in the pan on a low heat with just the water that is clinging to the leaves. When wilted, allow to cool and add to the egg mixture.
★ Place the rolled out pastry in the baking dish, fill with egg and spinach mixture.
★ Fold over the top of the pastry to seal it. Brush with milk and scatter with sesame seeds.
★ Bake in the middle shelf of the oven for 35 to 40 minutes.
★ Serve with a fresh salad.

# Resisting Temptation Hints

## Compare Biscuits

Addicted to biscuits? Try reading the nutritional information on the packet before you buy. For instance, did you know that one digestive biscuit has over 3g fat? If you're a digestive fan, I suggest try a different biscuit. Fig rolls are the champion of sweet biscuits, and even rich tea have less than half the fat of digestives.

## Get on the Wagon

I recommend everyone try an alcohol free week each month. For a couple of reasons – to love your liver, and for social butterflies, to get out of the habit of ordering alcoholic drinks when you go out. Alcohol is full of sneaky calories, and cutting out booze is an easy way to trim the waistline.

Stock up on juice and fizzy water prior to the week so you'll always have something nice to drink. Red grape juice served in a wine glass is a healthy substitute for it's alcoholic equivalent and you may not even notice the difference. In a sociable situation, soda water with freshly squeezed wedges of lime is a sophisticated alternative.

## Improve Your Energy Levels

Coffee a.k.a. 'rocket fuel' can have an evil knock on effect. Whilst it feels like it's boosting your energy levels in the short term, in the long term it may sap them. Did you know that adrenaline is released into your system when you drink caffeine? Adrenaline is responsible for your 'fight or flight' response, not really something you need sitting at a desk.

Quite often busy folk will drink a strong cup of coffee with breakfast, then complain of mid morning energy dip and needing a boost, i.e. another coffee often accompanied with a high GI snack, like a biscuit. This in turn creates another energy peak, then a sudden drop.

It is exhausting to continue through the day like this, so give your system a break by giving caffeine a body swerve... If you really can't live without coffee, try waiting until just after lunch and have one really good cup of freshly brewed coffee. You will experience the dip later on in the day and will be less likely to combat it with more caffeine.

# Fad or Fab

## A Good Donut

It's good to stay hydrated whilst out exercising, however holding a bulky drink bottle whilst running can compromise your running style as it creates tension through the shoulder. So, is it worth splashing out on a fancy water bottle? In a word, yes! A donut water bottle is much easier to hold and therefore causes less strain to travel up the arm into the shoulder. If you're doing a short run, you're probably better off drinking water before and after rather than carrying a bottle. If you like to drink on the go, then this is the one for you.

## Use Your Noodle

Aqua aerobics is a much underrated form of exercise. Don't underestimate how many calories you can burn with a really good water workout. If you're working out in the water, it makes sense to add some resistance. Foam dumbbells come in all shapes and sizes, but the most versatile piece of kit in the pool is the humble foam noodle. Costing just a few quid, you can do a whole host of exercises, from chest pressing to tummy exercises whilst floating on the noodle, to balance exercises standing on the noodle. Exercise in water is easy on the joints and great for older folk and those recovering from injury. In fact, I suggest exercise in water for anyone recovering from a lower body injury (or knee problem) as the water is buoyant and you can still get a good upper body workout without compromising the injury. Fabbo!

## Running Reading

After a dinner party one evening, we were talking good books. As we were leaving, our hosts Neil and Kim handed me the book *Born to Run* by Christopher McDougall. It's part adventure novel, part running book, about a lost tribe of Mexican Indians who live in a canyon and happen to be amazing ultra runners (that's ultra long distance, running over a marathon at a time). Not only is it an inspirational yarn, but also an informative book, and it touches on an alternative way of running. Naturally.

Before reading *Born to Run*, I read *Chi Running* which is a method of running developed by American ultra-marathoner Danny Dreyer based on the gentle philosophy of Tai Chi. It teaches you how to enjoy the process of training, focussing on good posture and a free and easy running style. It's based on core muscle strength as well as self-awareness, which will help you run better and avoid injuries. Go for it!

## Exercise of the Month

Skipping is a very effective method of getting your heart rate up. It takes a little practice (or remembering, if you used to skip rope at school), but it is well worth the patience as you master different moves.

You will either need to find a spot inside with a high ceiling and nothing breakable nearby, or a flat spot outside on tarmac, perhaps in a park. Putting on some fast-paced music can help you keep time.

1. Jog on the spot for a minute to warm up and to set your skipping pace.
2. Start skipping on alternating feet. It's like jogging on the spot, with the only difference of jogging over the swinging rope.
3. Aim to do one minute's skipping without a break, and build up with practice.
4. Vary your skipping by:
   * Jumping with both feet together
   * Hopping twice on one leg, then the other
   * Travelling forwards and backwards
   * Jumping from side to side, as if skiing
   * Skipping backwards

# Articles of the Month

## Decisions, Decisions

When I started my fitness business I was determined to name it 'Damage Control'. I had even designed a logo. I was advised by many people that this was a very silly idea and consequently now have a much more sensible business name.

However the idea of 'damage control' really is the motivation for many folk who make the decision to live a little healthier. It's the thought of what they don't want to look like that is often the proverbial kick up the ass. A more effective motivator is if they imagined what they would like to look like. It's easy to run away from a negative image, but you then need a positive projection to move towards. Can you imagine driving a car, knowing that you definitely wanted to avoid all roadworks, but you didn't have a positive idea of where you actually wanted to go? You would probably end up driving in circles.

Every day you make hundreds, if not thousands of decisions that affect your well being. To hit the snooze button? Spend time eating breakfast? Darn it, no time to walk to work now, it's on the bus. Go for that quadruple caramel crapaccino? Work through lunch? Forgot to pack lunch so it's a bacon butty? Quality Street? It would be rude to say no, or would it? Pub after work? Or work 'til late? Decisions, decisions, and you may not even be aware that you are making them.

Many decisions are informed by habit, some by peer pressure, perceived or otherwise, others are not even considered fully. So let's look a little at the process behind some of the choices you make each day and how to easily choose a little healthier.

Do you eat breakfast? A good many people do not, or say they do, but not until they get to work. BREAKFAST IS VERY IMPORTANT! The first step to having an easy day is to have a good hearty breakfast as soon as you can after waking up (in bed is fine, if you can arrange that). The reason for this is that it kickstarts your metabolism. You have effectively fasted for eight hours or more, so to break that fast and let your body know that it's ready for action is crucial. If you delay your first meal of the day, your body 'thinks' it's still in starvation (fasting) mode and so your metabolism will slow down to conserve calories. So to starve yourself in the morning is totally counter productive. Enjoy porridge! Or my warmer weather favourite, good quality raw muesli with fresh berries and natural yoghurt. Feast like a king in the morning.

If you work in an office, your day will invariably involve co-workers thrusting chocolate and sweeties at you. I dare you to decline. If you have eaten in the morning, you will not be so hungry for such sugary nonsense. Eating more food earlier in the day helps avoid an energy dip in the afternoon and the temptation to scoff on high energy junk.

In addition to this, you will also have more energy. This is a surprisingly common reason people state for starting up a fitness programme. You would think that if you used more energy you would have less energy, but the reverse is true. "How can this be so?" You ask. Expending energy is a bit like momentum. Once you get going and feel great for it, you gather momentum (and get fitter so can go faster anyway). Going back to nutrition, if you eat well early in the day you will also have more energy. You're more likely to want to go for a brisk walk at lunch and come back feeling invigorated, ready for the afternoon and your working day will fly by. If you find it difficult to stick to exercising, find a friend who's happy to meet up with you and go for an after work walk, run, bike ride or game of football. Have a regular night that you meet and then the decision of what you do with some summery evenings is already pre-arranged. Rope in different mates and have a whole social calendar of activities to look forward to each week. Getting outdoors and in shape should be something to look forward to, and then the decision to actually do it becomes a 'no brainer'.

Decisions become easy. Rather than avoiding things you don't want, think about the things that you do want to do. And they will come to you... Or you will get to them... You just need a plan.

## Energy: You know you want it, but how do you get it?

It's amazing that in this day and age of convenience and time saving devices that people complain of having a lack of energy. It's easy to revert to being a couch potato, but it's such a waste of life.

There are a few crucial components that contribute to how energetic you feel: rest, nutrition and outlook. Here are some ideas to put some zip in your life.

**Rest:** A strangely often overlooked factor, rest is crucial to all beings. Our muscles repair themselves and our brains process information during sleep, so if you're lethargic – sleep more! Or even try an afternoon 20 minute power nap when you can... Is your bedding comfortable? Sometimes a new pillow can do wonders.

You may like to switch off mobile phones, wi-fi and any other electrical equipment to ensure a better night's sleep.

If you suffer from insomnia, try writing a list of all the things you have to do the next day so you can relax without lots of thoughts whirling around your head. A nice hot bath and a sleepytime tea can help.

**Nutrition:** Always eat a decent sized slow-burning breakfast. It's essential to eat as early in the day as you can to kick start your metabolism. Also try a healthy mid morning snack so you aren't tempted by junk food at lunch. A good Vitamin B Complex tablet may also help energy levels.

Eat lots of raw, unprocessed nutrient dense foods. Enjoy raw salads for the goodness they provide. I always feel better after a bowl of leaves… Drink around two litres of water a day to flush the toxins from your system. You may go to the loo more, but you will also have clearer skin.

Resist caffeine, as it can seriously mess with your energy levels. If you are going to indulge, make it good quality caffeine (i.e. dark chocolate or freshly brewed coffee) and have it once a day to prevent the cyclical nature of energy dips and peaks.

**Outlook:** This basically covers everything else. Your mental outlook is a crucial component of your verve levels. Take time away from your computer (even at work) and get outside whenever possible. It's thought that a little time outdoors every day can significantly boost mood and well being. Get your heart rate up and breathe deeply – you'll increase both your oxygen intake as well as endorphins. Yoga and swimming are both energising activities to try. I truly believe that energy creates energy – being more energetic pays dividends and you will feel more lively for it…

# The Humble History of the Hula Hoop

Hula hoops are back! It's official... Hula-ing is the next fitness craze. I for one am more than happy to jump on the bandwagon. Spinning a humble hoop around one's waist is a fabulous way to trim and tone wobbly belly bits. But where did it all begin?

Around 3,000 years ago, Egyptians made hoops out of grape vines and propelled them along the ground with sticks. In ancient Greece hooping was recommended for weight loss. In 14th century England, hooping was popular but then discouraged as it was blamed it for heart attacks and back dislocations. The word "hula" was added in the early 18th century as sailors returning from Hawaii noticed the similarity between hula dancing and hooping.

In 1957 the hula hoop was reinvented in the US by the Wham-O toy company. Of course they tried to patent it, but as it was such an ancient concept, the most they could do was trademark it. This was enough, and the humble hula hoop went on to sell 100 million in just two years. See the Coen brothers brilliant film *The Hudsucker Proxy* for 1950's hooping references and the classic line "You know, for kids!"

As a child, hula hooping was one of the best bits of my lunchtime. So it was with genuine joy that I realised that hula hoops have made a comeback... for adults! See www.hooping.org for more information and also how to make your own hoop. The workout hoop I use is heavier and bigger than the children's lightweight (and tiny) hoops that you find in toy shops.

Perhaps we should look to children's activities more for workout inspiration, as skipping and trampolining are also great workouts. Not only are they effective pulse raising (cardiovascular) workouts, they are also fun.

# JUNE

June is a great month for fitness... The weather is warm, the days at the longest and people are out and about. This is my favourite time of the year, when Edinburgh really comes to life. If you are training for an event, remember to slowly increase your distance with training.

## WHAT'S IN SEASON

It's nearing peak growing season, so here's what you might find locally:

**Artichokes, asparagus, aubergine, broad beans, carrots, cauliflower, cherries, courgettes, elderflowers, gooseberries, lovage, mint, new carrots, new potatoes, parsley, peas, radishes, raspberries, rhubarb, rocket (easy to grow in a window box), tayberries, strawberries, sorrel, spinach, spring onions.**

## OATCAKE TOPPING OF THE MONTH

Let's salsa baby! Whether you make your own or buy it ready made, salsa is the lowest fat dip around, and some can have a real kick to get you going. Whenever buying dips, check the fat content as they can vary wildly – from about 1% fat for salsa to 45% for nacho cheese dip. Consider yourself warned.

# Easy Summer Recipes

## Oh So Easy Omelette

Omelettes are a quick and easy dinner that can use up leftovers from your fridge. As an added bonus they taste nice cold the next day for lunch. A broad definition of an omelette is 'a beaten egg dish, cooked in a frying pan'. So there's loads of scope for invention. I rarely measure out my omelette ingredients. Rather, I prepare a chopping board of ingredients and mix with eggs that have been beaten and seasoned. Sometimes I also add some milk to the egg mixture, for a lighter omelette texture.

Here's my foolproof method to invent your own omelette.

4 – 6 organic free-range eggs
Tiny pinch sea salt, and ground black pepper
Chopped herbs (parsley, basil, thyme, rosemary)

★ Beat the eggs in a jug, mix with the chopped herbs and season. Set aside.

Two handfuls of a combination of:

Garlic cloves, crushed
Onions (any type), chopped
Mushrooms, sliced
Spinach, wilted
Red or green peppers, finely chopped
Butternut squash, cubed and gently roasted, or steamed
Tinned sweetcorn kernels
Feta cheese, cubed
Toasted pine nuts

★ On a medium heat, sauté garlic and onions in a tbsp of olive oil. Add any vegetables that you'd like to brown. Make sure there is enough oil to coat the pan, but it doesn't need to be swimming in it.
★ When the vegetables are softish, pour in the egg mixture and lower the heat.
★ Aim to cook the egg through. You can either flip it over, or fold it in half (perhaps with a wee bit of cheese in the middle), or pop it under the grill to brown the top. The grill option is my personal favourite as my omelettes tend to turn into scrambled eggs if I try to turn them over.
★ Serve with a fresh garden salad.

# Spanish Omelette

Protein is an important element of any diet, and even more so if you are exercising regularly – it's the building block of muscle and tissue and is required to help the body repair itself. The humble egg has had some bad press, however is a great source of protein, especially for vegetarians. This omelette is perfect for four people, or for two for dinner and lunch.

700g potatoes, scrubbed, skins on
1 red onion (or a brown onion, or one leek), chopped
1 tbsp olive oil
1 clove garlic, crushed
2 tbsp chopped fresh parsley (or you can use mixed dried herbs)
4 organic free-range eggs
100ml milk
60g grated cheese (optional)
Ground black pepper

★ In a jug, whisk the eggs together with the milk, black pepper and most of the parsley. Set aside.

★ Wash and chop the potatoes into thin slices. Use fresh good quality waxy potatoes and leave the skin on. Par boil / steam / microwave until they are slightly cooked, but still firm. Drain.

★ Heat the oil in a non-stick frying pan over a medium heat and sauté onion and garlic until transparent, add the potato and cook for a few minutes.

★ Turn the heat down to medium low, add the egg mixture and cook until omelette starts solidifying and browns on the bottom.

★ Sprinkle on the grated cheese and the rest of the parsley and pop the pan under a grill to brown the top. Wrap some tinfoil around the frying pan handle to stop it burning under the grill.

★ Serve with rocket salad.

## Rocket Salad

Rocket leaves have recently become a common sight in our shops, and are full of iron and nutrients. You can grow rocket easily in a window box, and it will provide you with fresh leaves for about a month. One of the stronger tasting salad leaves around, they're also versatile for use in cooking (wilted rocket with pasta, garlic, a little olive oil and pine nuts is a divine and easy dinner).

Colander full of rocket leaves, rinsed and drained
Handful of cherry tomatoes, halved
Some pine nuts, lightly toasted (optional)
Balsamic vinegar
Olive / rapeseed oil

★ Toss all in a bowl and drizzle with a splash of balsamic vinegar and a tiny bit of good quality oil.

★ Other additions could include roast garlic, roast red peppers, olives or some shaved parmesan cheese.

# Unusual Things to do with Fruit

Not as it sounds – this is the season to buy tropical fruit. I always have good fruity intentions but sometimes fruit sits in the bowl until past it's best. Here are some ideas of how to rescue over-ripe pineapple, mango or avocado.

## Mauritian Pineapple

So you've bought a pineapple and let it over-ripen. A lovely way to enjoy this (high GI) fruit is to chop it up and sprinkle it with chilli flakes and a tiny pinch of sea salt. I tried this first from a roadside vendor in Mauritius and it's a taste sensation.

## Mango Lassi

This time you've bought a mango, and it's got a bit too ripe (or maybe it's even a bit stringy). No fear, zizz it with same amount of natural yoghurt and a splash of OJ and you've got a tropical lassi.

## Grilled Avocado

In the immortal words of Monty Python "and now for something completely different": cut an avocado in half and de-stone. Place skin side up and grill for a few minutes, then skin side down and grill for a few more minutes. Serve with a splash of balsamic vinegar and ground pepper, or lemon juice if you prefer.

# Resisting Temptation Hints of the month

## Avoid Hunger

Resisting temptation is not a problem if you're not hungry in the first place. At lunchtime many people fall into the grip of crisps or chocolate. For most, the simple reason is that they are hungry. Simple as that. Try having a healthy mid morning snack. Some oatcakes or a small handful of raw nuts and seeds will keep your metabolism ticking over and also ensure that you are not ravenous at lunch (and therefore are less likely to make unwise food decisions). Easy!

## It's OK to be Fussy

Are you someone who doesn't like to cause a scene? Most of us are, and can find making healthy choices whilst eating out a challenging experience. It's one of the most common excuses for not sticking to healthy eating. It's OK to ask waiters if a pasta sauce is creamy or not, it's OK to ask for salad dressing on the side rather than all over the salad, it's OK to order a starter sized main course, it's OK to be fussy. Your body is a temple, as they say, so it's OK to care about what you put into it. Just because you're eating out doesn't mean you need to completely abandon good intentions. I find that most waiters are incredibly patient when I ask them about what's in their dishes. They may even prepare you something special 'off menu'.

## Be Accountable

A food diary is a very effective way to trace what you're eating and how much – writing it down means you're accountable for what you put in your mouth. There are also various new mobile apps, which are handy for keeping your food diary up to date.

# Fad or Fab

## Pilates Bodycircles

HaB are a brand that produces some high quality goods. Their Bodycircles are most certainly high quality, but also pretty pointless. The premise is to tone arms by twirling these weighted hoops around the forearms. You might remember doing this at school with a hula hoop. The idea is the same, but the hoops are smaller. So small in fact, that the only thing they're good for is twirling around your arms. So when you get bored of this (for me, after five minutes), the reason for owning these mini hoops becomes redundant. Hula hoops, yes, arm hoops, a big fat fad!

## Skinfold Callipers

Skinfold callipers are a low tech, but accurate way of measuring your percentage of body fat. They look like big pincers and they measure the thickness of pinches of flesh on four specific sites of the body. By measuring subcutaneous body fat (i.e. fat just beneath the skin) you can work out body fat as a percentage of your mass.

From working out your percentage of body fat, you can then calculate what percentage body fat you need to be healthy, and then how much weight you need to lose to become the shape you want to be. I find skinfold callipers to be more reliable than the more modern Bioelectrical Impedance Monitor (that puts a very small electrical current through your body to measure resistance, and therefore, body fat).

Bioelectrical Impedance testing is meant to be the way forward in the fitness industry, but there are major issues. For an accurate measurement, the person has to abstain from caffeine and alcohol for 24 hours and have 'normal' hydration. The test needs to be done at the same time of day each time and under exactly the same circumstances. I have had wildly varying results over the course of a week (plus or minus 6% fat), which is an issue that I have never encountered using the old fashioned skinfold callipers. So I have reverted to using the 'old school' skinfold callipers. Sometimes simple is best.

## Exercise of the Month

So what exactly is interval training? It's a training method used by professional athletes to increase stamina and speed. If you imagine a running track, a middle-distance athlete would perhaps sprint the straights and recover on the corners. Their heart rate drops down before being pushed back up again on the straights. This allows the athlete to train for longer, harder and more effectively. Recovery is always an important part of any exercise programme, and by exerting yourself, then letting yourself recover before trying again, you can get some fantastic results.

# Articles of the Month

## Cardiovascular Fitness: What's in it for me?

Cardiovascular (or cardio) fitness refers to the kind of exercise where you get active and raise your heart rate. By raising your heart rate, you are effectively exercising your heart. Your heart is an amazing collection of muscles, throughout your life it is responsible for the circulation of freshly oxygenated blood to your entire body. Your body tissue requires oxygen to function, and your heart is the pump that gets it there. If you imagine your heart as a muscle, you can easily understand why you need to exercise it.

By going for a fast walk / jog / cycle you increase your bodies oxygen requirement, therefore your heart needs to pump faster. This is why your heart rate increases when you exercise. By raising your heart rate to a safe but effective level, you can train your heart to work more efficiently. The outcome? A fitter, stronger heart with an increased output; overall a healthier organ with a lower resting heart rate (as your heart is working better, so needs to pump less). Cardio exercise also helps to increase the capacity and effectiveness of your lungs, and can help to lower blood pressure.

Cardiovascular exercise can also help speed up your metabolism, which is great news for burning calories easier. So how much is enough? It is recommended that we all undertake cardio exercise for at least 30 minutes on a minimum of three days per week. Of course, it is always possible to do longer, and 30 minutes is really a bare minimum (for example an aerobics class usually lasts 45 to 60 minutes).

## Move and Feel Happy

Exercise makes you feel happy. It's proven and it's true. It's one of the easiest and cheapest ways to boost your mood. Have you ever been for a walk up a big hill and remember the feeling when you got to the top? Elation? Exhaustion? Satisfaction?

When you exercise, various feel good neurotransmitters are pinged around your brain. It's a similar reaction to eating lots of chocolate – the endorphins, including serotonin and dopamine (the same stuff that's released by morphine) are the 'pleasure principle'.

These feel good neurotransmitters are released after undertaking cardiovascular exercise, such as running. You need to reach a certain level of exertion for these neurotransmitters to be released. So why is exercise not more addictive? Some would argue it is, and I am sure you will know someone who has been hooked on exercise.

Whatever the reason for the release of these neurotransmitters, it has been shown that physically active people recover from mild depression more quickly. In fact I have found that if someone is feeling blue, getting them outside for a long brisk walk or jog really helps turn their mood around. I feel this is a combination of both the body's reaction to exercise and also the change of scenery. In Edinburgh it's easy to find some green space, even in the most built up areas, and just being outside and getting extra oxygen moving around the body creates a noticeable shift in mood.

Add to this, I find creativity is heightened by a good bout of cardio exercise. If I'm ever stuck on writing an article, I put it aside until I've been out for a bike ride. If you'd like to read an excellent book relating to exercise and creativity, try the best-selling Japanese author Haruki Murakami's excellent memoir *Things That I Talk About When I Talk About Running*, where he links the concentration required for his work as a prolific novelist, and his daily hour-long runs.

Whatever way you look at it, pulse-raising exercise in any form is something that your body benefits from on both a physical and emotional level. So if you're waiting for inspiration, wait no more!

# Protein: Your Body's Pro-Team... Not just for Body Builders

If it weren't for protein, you wouldn't exist. Your skin, blood cells, muscles, hair and bones all contain some form of protein. Protein is essential to keep your body functioning normally, for growth, repair and even to form neurotransmitters that tell your body what to do, and when. Protein is made of strings of amino acids, which are the basic building blocks. There are nine essential amino acids (that you need to get from food) and thirteen non-essential (that you can manufacture yourself from non-protein food sources). If you imagine that your muscle cells are about 22% protein, you can understand why you need to get enough. This is why many body-builders can be somewhat obsessed with protein shakes and the like. They need protein to build their muscles. The good news is a healthy balanced diet will provide you with all the protein you need. The average adult needs about 0.8g of protein per kilogram of body weight, however you will need more if you are exercising or recovering from injury (to help build new muscle tissue).

Animal sources provide the most biologically similar form of protein for humans. The higher the biological value (b.v.), the easier it can be used by the body. An egg has the b.v. of 100% and is known as a complete protein; however it is not only animal-derived foods that contain useable protein. The humble soya bean is an excellent source of protein, and soy products can be a valuable source of protein for vegetarians. If you're not a tofu fan, don't despair, you can obtain protein from vegetable sources. Other vegetarian sources often contain incomplete proteins, meaning that they may lack one or more essential amino acids. To boost the protein value, it can be combined with another food that is rich in the missing amino acid. Some examples are:

★ Whole grains and legumes: dhal and rice, beans on toast, felafel and pita bread.
★ Whole grains and dairy products: a simple cheese sandwich, pasta and parmesan, porridge with milk (breakfast of champions!)
★ Dairy products and legumes: baked beans with cheese
★ Dairy products with nuts or seeds: muesli and milk
★ Legumes with nuts or seeds: houmous made of chickpeas and tahini (sunflower seed paste)

# Why Detox?

A detox is where you aim to ingest fewer toxins through food and lifestyle. Every detox is different, and you can choose one to suit your own requirements. Detoxing helps to cleanse the system, reset habits and is a great way to kick-start weight loss. I detox if I find 'bad' habits creeping in.

An example of a detox is a month of no alcohol, meat, processed foods or chocolate. It's useful to view the period as a time where you get rid of redundant habits and replace them with new, healthier habits. Personally I like to 'ramp up' detoxing as my body adapts.

I usually enjoy a good cup of proper coffee each day, but I found it was creeping up to two or even three cups on a busy day. Apparently 90% of the world's adult population imbibes caffeinated drinks every day. So for a week I also cut out coffee. If you are a regular coffee drinker, the first couple days without caffeine can cause headaches, mood swings and irritability. I got all three symptoms, and was shocked that I was drinking enough caffeine to cause withdrawal headaches.

In the past I've tried brown rice detoxing, where you eat only brown rice and drink herbal tea for a few days. It's extreme but good for cleansing the system, the palate and the mind. I remember eating a Müller Light after a brown rice detox and being able to taste all the chemicals; it put me off Müller Light for life.

However you don't need to subsist only on brown rice to detox. There are many fruit and vegetable detoxes and juicing diets that are great at this time of year when there's nice stuff in season. You can simply try a weekend and make it your 'health spa' time. If you do detox, listen to your body. It depends on the individual as to how you'll react to eliminating different food and drink from your diet. Weakness and tiredness from extreme detoxes can happen, but the end result is that you have healthier habits in place (and you may even lose a bit of body fat). Remember that although detoxes should be short term with an end date in mind, they can have long-term positive benefits.

# JULY

It's getting to that summer holiday time of year. It's a great time to plan a fitness programme you can do if you're going away. Whether you're swimming in a hotel pool, splashing along a beach or striding up a Scottish hill, summer really is the time to be active.

## WHAT'S IN SEASON

**Aubergine, asparagus, beans, cabbage, carrots, celery, cherries, cauliflower, fennel, gooseberries, herbs, kohlrabi (lovely grated on salad), loganberries, lettuce, mangetout, nectarines, new potatoes, oyster mushrooms, peas, peaches, radishes, raspberries, rhubarb, rocket, strawberries, spinach, tomatoes, watercress.**

## OATCAKE TOPPING OF THE MONTH

Roast a whole aubergine in the oven at 200°C, turning occasionally, until it collapses. Leave to cool, then peel the skin off. Mash the aubergine flesh with a drizzle of olive oil, and blend by hand until creamy in texture. The resulting dip is delicious on oatcakes, and one aubergine worth of dip will last you a whole week.

# Easy Summer Recipes

## Customising Bread Maker Bread

Summer may not seem the appropriate season to discuss bread making, however one of my favourite summer meals is a big salad served with a wedge of home made bread. It's a meal in itself. Ditch that awful supermarket stuff (how can bread last for a week? What do they put in it?) and eat proper bread.

I've recently started to experiment more with the bread maker, exploring different flavours and textures. My original bread maker recipe book didn't have a recipe for rye bread, so here's one I've adapted.

*Ingredients – Large loaf measurements indicated (medium loaf in brackets)*
370 ml water (300ml)
10ml lemon juice (10ml)
30ml sunflower oil (22ml)
175g rye flour (125g)
500g unbleached white bread flour (375g)
2 tbsp skimmed milk powder (1.5 tbsp)
2 tsp salt (1.5 tsp)
4 tsp brown sugar (1 tbsp)
1.5 tsp easy blend dried yeast (1tsp)

*Optional – add a variety of:*
caraway seeds
sunflower seeds
small handful oats (for a crunchy crust)
lemon rind
fresh herbs
garlic

★ Add the liquid to the bread pan.
★ Sprinkle over the flours and flavourings.
★ In separate corners, add the skimmed milk powder, sugar and salt.
★ Make a well in the middle, but not as far down as the liquid, and add the yeast.
★ Set the bread machine to basic / normal setting, dark crust.

# Aubergine, Halloumi and Mint Stacks

*Serves two*

1 clove garlic, crushed

1 tbsp light soy sauce

3 tbsp balsamic vinegar

3 tbsp olive oil

1 medium aubergine, sliced 5 mm thick

1 packet halloumi (approx 200g), sliced 5 mm thick

2 tbsp fresh mint, chopped

★ Combine the top four ingredients in a jug to make the marinade.

★ Arrange the sliced aubergine on a deep plate.

★ Pour the marinade over the sliced aubergine and let sit for 45 minutes.

★ Heat a heavy bottom frying pan and shake each piece of aubergine before placing into the pan. Fit as much in the pan as you can, the slices will shrink as they're cooked.

★ Cook for 3 – 4 minutes on each side.

★ Remove from pan and pile them up and cover with foil to keep warm.

★ Place the sliced halloumi in the pan, without oil (it shouldn't stick if you move it around).

★ Cook for 3 – 4 minutes on each side, until golden

★ Alternate layers of aubergine and halloumi, pour over the remaining marinade, and scatter with chopped mint.

*Note*: Try a handful of cherry tomatoes per person to serve dotted on the plate – these cut through the richness of the aubergine.

# Sushi, a Healthy Lunch Alternative

Nori sushi rolls are deceptively easy to make and look dead fancy. Here's a step by step guide to producing your own Japanese delicacies. The nori seaweed wrapper is a rich source of calcium, zinc and iodine. The fillings are as healthy as you like, from the veggies listed below to fresh raw fish from the fishmonger, just make sure it's very fresh. All of the specialised ingredients can be found in a Chinese supermarket.

*Serves four*

   1 packet sushi nori – sheets of toasted seaweed
   ¼ cup seasoned rice vinegar*
   1½ cups sushi rice
   1 tube wasabi – green Japanese horseradish
   Light soy sauce, for dipping
   Pickled ginger, for serving
   Bamboo rolling mat
   Fillings: avocado, carrot, cucumber, Japanese yellow radish or very fresh salmon, halibut or tuna

   * be sure it's the seasoned type or you need to add sugar and salt yourself

*To make the rice*

★ Add the rice to 1¾ cups of cold water and bring to a boil.
★ Reduce to the lowest heat and simmer, covered, for 20 minutes or until all water is absorbed.
★ Remove from heat and let stand, covered, for 10 minutes.
★ Turn rice into a large non-metal bowl. Drizzle seasoned rice vinegar over the rice and gently combine, then cover.
★ Whilst you're waiting for the rice to cool, finely chop your ingredients into long sticks.

*Now the fun bit, the rolling*

★ Lay a sheet of sushi nori onto the bamboo mat.
★ Spread a thin layer of the rice evenly on the sheet, leaving an inch free on the furthest side from you.
★ Place your filling ingredients horizontally about one inch from the beginning of the rice.
★ You can spread some wasabi next to the filling to add extra bite.
★ Slightly dampen the exposed nori, then roll the mat.
★ Top tip: The rice is sticky, so keep a bowl of water handy so you can easily clean your fingers and dampen implements when required.
★ Slice into approx 8 rolls using a wet sharp knife.
★ Present your rolls on a tray with a dipping bowl of light soy sauce, a small mound of wasabi and pickled ginger on the side.
★ The more you practise nori rolls, the easier it gets.

# Quick and Easy Spanish Salad

*Combine the chickpeas in this recipe with wholegrain pita bread and you have a complete vegetable protein. It's tasty, really easy and keeps in the fridge well for the next day.*

*Serves four as a side salad*

1 tin chickpeas, drained and rinsed
3 medium tomatoes, chopped
½ – 1 red onion, finely chopped
Couple handfuls of rocket
Handful of flat leaf parsley, chopped (you can also use fresh mint)
½ lemon, juiced
Drizzle olive oil
Freshly ground pepper to taste

★ Combine everything in a salad bowl.
★ You can also add other salad ingredients such as finely chopped peppers, chilli, cucumber, or feta cheese.

# Avocado, Fennel and Orange Salad

*A truly blissful combination*

1 avocado, cubed
1 fennel bulb, very finely sliced
1 orange, chopped

★ Combine all ingredients. You can add a bit of the fennel fronds for an interesting look. If you mash up the avocado a bit, it makes the salad nice and creamy.

# Resisting Temptation Hints of the Month

## Set the Breakfast Table

Breakfast is the most important meal of your day, but sadly the mostly missed meal of the day. During busy periods I quite often finish work quite late at night and it takes a while to relax. As part of my routine, I pretend I run a Bed and Breakfast and prepare my table for breakfast (those with children may joke that they do run a B and B). Lay out placemats, empty bowls, glasses and cutlery. Try arranging the cereal boxes artfully on the table if you've got a spare minute. In the morning when you wander into the kitchen, breakfast is already laid out ready to go. It also makes mornings feel more organised and you can start the day on top of the world.

## Summer Solutions

It's easy to use summer holidays as an opportunity to eat healthily. The weather is warm, lovely fruit and veg is in season and it's the time to eat light and nutritious grub. If you're on holiday use your break to get into good eating habits. If you're going to a BBQ, take your own healthy options for the grill. Corn cobs, red pepper, big mushrooms, freshly caught fish and Quorn burgers come up lovely on the ol' hot plate, and means you can avoid the usual suspects of sausages, fatty meat and white bread. If you're abroad, try foods you've never tried before – be a culinary adventurer.

## Brush Your Teeth

If you're prone to snacking late at night, try brushing your teeth a couple of hours before you go to bed. You'll need to brush your teeth again if you want a snack…

# Fad or Fab

## EasyTone Trainers

Shoes that can make you fitter? That's the claim from Reebok and a growing number of shoe brands. I've tried on some goofy boots (MBTs) before, but finally bit the bullet and invested in a pair of Reebok EasyTone trainers. These retro looking trainers can be thought of as 'effort shoes' (i.e. they require extra effort). As sceptical as I was, the 'balance pod' soles mean that legs work harder to keep you upright. Imagine walking everywhere in cleated cycling shoes and you get the idea. Not recommended for running but an interesting addition to the wardrobe. A tentative fab, but remember posture, posture posture.

## Sports Drinks

There's a huge variety of sports drinks on the market, but are they really necessary? If you are a moderate exerciser and your sessions are an hour or under, the truth is that you may not need them. Plain water is best to sip on whilst exercising. Also be sure that you are adequately hydrated before and after a session.

If you are running long distance, doing an extended hill walk, long bike ride, or are exercising in the heat you may find a drink containing some sugar (carbohydrate) helpful. This is because fluid with a similar carbohydrate concentration to blood is absorbed more easily by the stomach, thereby hydrating you better. Rather than spend money on fancy drinks, often containing aspartame, try a squeeze of fresh lime or lemon, or even weak ribena in your drink bottle. This is especially handy in hot weather. For those watching their waistlines, remember sugary drinks contain calories. Our Western diet tends to be high in salt, so salt replacement is not that high on the agenda. If you feel you could benefit from an 'electrolyte replacement system', add a tiny wee pinch of sea salt to your drink bottle, only a tiny bit is required so you won't taste it.

A word on drink bottles, get a proper sports bottle so you can keep it very clean in a dishwasher or washed by hand at a high temperature. That's my final thought before I give sports drinks the thumbs down for most of us. Don't believe the faddish hype.

# Powerbreathe

I had heard brilliant things about the Powerbreathe device before recommending it to my clients. It looks like an oversize asthma inhaler and it works by training the muscles that assist inspiration (breathing). These are the intercostal muscles that expand the rib cage, increasing the lung volume; stronger muscles mean they creating more of a pressure difference, it means a deeper breath. It can also help asthma.

I was impressed when one client stopped wheezing and cut about 10% from her run time – impressive, as her run was only 13 minutes long, so a decent improvement. And then another client cut 10% off her run time. It's an easy way you can train to run faster whilst sitting on the sofa. Fab.

# Exercise of the Month: Try a Tri

A triathlon involves a swim (in open water or in a pool), a cycle, then a run to finish. Relatively unknown in Scotland until only a few years ago, this is a fast-growing sport and not only for the ultra fit (thanks to the popularity of sprint distances). For example:

Sprint triathlons can vary in distance and start with a 400m – 750m swim, then a 6 -12 mile (10 – 20km) cycle finishing with a 3 – 6 mile (5 – 10 km) run.

Olympic distance is 750m swim, 24.8 mile (40km) cycle, finishing with a 6.2 mile (10km) run.

Iron man distance is 2.4 mile (3.8km) swim, 112 mile (180km) cycle, finishing with running a full marathon

As you can see, the distances vary, and there is one available to suit most fitness levels. See www.triathlonscotland.org for more info.

# July Articles

## Preparing for a Triathlon

Train for a triathlon as a competition of four parts, swimming, cycling, running and the transitions (where you go from pool to bike, and bike to running). If you ever watched triathlons on the telly you will have seen the athletes fly through their transitions, bike shoes already clipped onto bicycle pedals so it is just a matter of slipping their feet in and cycling off. For the amateur triathlete, especially in chilly Scotland, there is a whole dark art to completing a tri. Not only do you need to be relatively fit, but you need to be highly organised with the right kit.

Here are some essential components to be aware of:

★ Learn to put on a swimming cap, especially if you've never worn one. Often coloured coded swim caps identify the various swim heats.

★ Use a suitable bike. Many triathletes use road bikes, but you don't have to. Just be sure that your bike is serviced and running well before the race.

★ Source a bicycle rack for the car if you don't have one already.

★ Practise drying from the swim and putting cycling shoes (and socks) on wet feet. Getting changed in a hurry can save you valuable time.

★ Preparing a 'tri box' – a plastic crate into which you put everything you need for the race: goggles, towel, cycling / running shoes and clothes, bike helmet and gloves at the very least.

★ Familiarise yourself with the route if possible – it will make the race easier if you know where you are going.

★ Plan what to eat before and what food to take with you. I prefer natural honey shots to carb gels, but practice and decide what works best for you.

★ Prepare what to wear no matter the weather.

★ Take your own safety pins for race number, or invest in a 'tri-belt', a webbing belt onto which to clip the race number / carb gels for transition ease.

★ Learn how to 'rack' a bike in the race racks.

★ Not forgetting the actual training. Simulate the conditions as similarly as possible (i.e. running after cycling, cycling after swimming).

Careful planning is everything.

# Oatcakes are better than OK. OK?

Oatcakes are my favourite food for energy. As a mid-morning snack they can't be beat. I love oatcakes as they are (fairly obviously) a portable source of oats. I personally believe oats to be a very valuable cereal.

According to Wikipedia:

"Scottish soldiers in the 14th Century carried a metal plate and a sack of oatmeal. According to contemporary accounts, one would heat the plate over fire, moisten a bit of oatmeal and make a cake to comfort his stomach. Hence it is no marvel that the Scots should be able to make longer marches than other men."

Apparently oatcakes were originally baked by Romans who carried oats to plant wherever they went. Oats were one of the few cereals to flourish in northern Scotland and so consequently oatcakes became a staple of the Highlanders' diet (along with porridge). And a darn fine diet too…

Oatcakes are low on the Glycaemic Index, which means that they are 'slow burning' and will give you energy for longer. They keep you feeling fuller for longer, and so if you have a snack on oatcakes in the morning, come lunch time you're less likely to reach for junk food. They're brilliant for sustaining your energy levels and keeping your blood sugar level steady.

Add to this, oats are a good source of vitamin E, zinc, selenium, copper, iron, manganese, magnesium and protein and are also thought to help lower cholesterol. What more could you ask for from Scotland's national cereal?

Beware some luxury oatcakes are surprisingly high in fat, up to 4.5g of fat per oatcake – that's more than a chocolate digestive. Nairn's rough oatcakes are a good buy and are available everywhere, they're about a quid a box and clock in at a more reasonable 1.5g fat. As an added bonus they come in nifty little packets that fit easily in a handbag or briefcase.

The only problem with oatcakes is they leave crumbs in your keyboard if you eat them as you type.

## Why Yo-Yo Diets Don't Work

Want to lose weight quick? The unfortunate answer is that a 'quick fix' low calorie diet may work in the short term, but may end up with you ending up putting on more weight in the long run. Hence the term 'yo-yo dieting'.

In a nutshell, when you diet, your body 'thinks' it's starving. Our bodies are sophisticated creations and to understand how your metabolism works (how efficiently you burn calories), you need to think back to primitive times. Back in the day when food was scarce, if we 'dieted' it was involuntary and due to a shortage of food. As the body had less fuel to operate on, it would switch into 'efficient' mode, and metabolism slowed down to last longer over the period of starvation. In this situation, the body also learns to store calories as fat reserves for later, in case the famine continues. Think of animals in hibernation, when their metabolism slows right down so they can survive through winter.

Our lifestyles have evolved radically and us lucky folk generally don't suffer food shortages. However our biological systems have taken longer to adapt. So even though we may know that we are dieting (deliberately starving) ourselves to get thinner, our bodies 'think' "I have to slow down my processing to make this food last". So you may lose some weight in the short term (quite often water if you're on a high protein low carb diet), but as soon as your eating habits return to normal you will just put the weight back on, and then some. Your metabolism will have slowed down due to dieting, so you will store more calories as body fat.

This is a very simplified outline of why restricted calorie dieting in the short term will not do you any favours in the long term. It is very possible to tone up in a month, however significant permanent weight loss requires a more sensible and controlled approach to both nutrition and exercise.

## The Perils of Overtraining

A good exercise programme should get you fitter and also help you remain injury free. Remaining injury free is crucial in any exercise programme. So it's important to ramp up intensity as the individual's fitness level improves. The body adapts to exercise by burning body fat and building muscle, and it does this best with incremental change (combined with a corresponding nutritional programme).

Scheduled rest days are crucial to allow the body to recover from exercise. Muscle builds by experiencing tiny rips and tears with exercise. You develop muscular strength due to the subsequent healing of these muscle fibres, bigger and stronger than before. Your body is adapting to exercise. If you don't have a day off, then it doesn't have a chance to heal before you are working it again. Regular exercise at an appropriate level with rest days is the most reliable method to use. An injured body will not want to continue a fitness programme.

# Do You Work Through Injury?

It is very frustrating when you build up a good level of fitness and then get injured, especially as the most effective road to recovery is rest. It is still possible to maintain a level of fitness, however allowing the injury to recover should be top priority. My hints for returning from injury:

★ For sprains and strains, apply a cool compress as soon as possible. Remember the First Aid mantra R.I.C.E. – rest, ice, compression, elevation. Applied straight away this can help prevent the injury worsening.

★ Rest the injury: You may need to rearrange your life to accommodate this. Try to rest the injury as much as possible, don't be tempted to train through the pain.

★ Pain is the body's way of telling you that something is wrong. Listen to it.

★ Get extra sleep: The body repairs itself when you are asleep, so what better reason for getting an hour or two's extra kip? An afternoon nap, if you are able, can do wonders. Alternatively, be sure to get to bed extra early whilst recovering.

★ Eat well: Extra protein and hydration will help the body repair itself. Make sure you eat a least five fresh fruit and veg a day (more is good). You can add in a multivitamin, just in case. If you're feeling drained, try a good vitamin B complex supplement.

★ Follow instructions: I highly recommend going to a private physiotherapist for the treatment of sports injuries. Yes, it costs extra, but otherwise you'll be waiting six weeks or more on the NHS. Immediate treatment saves time and speeds up recovery. Be sure to follow their advice.

★ You might need to change the kind of exercise you do. Many folk get lower leg injuries from imbalances when running on tarmac. Swap it for something low impact. Try working out in water, it cushions the body wonderfully and has a cooling effect. Water physiotherapy (hydrotherapy) is being used more widely in Australia and it's only a matter of time until it's used here. You can exercise around the injury, but be aware of how the injured part may be affected.

★ Give yourself time: It can be frustrating waiting for the body to recover, but essential. Give yourself extra time to do the everyday things in life – even simple things like getting from point A to B might take longer. The more patient you are, the quicker you will heal. For long term conditions, this can be frustrating, especially if you find yourself putting on weight and losing muscle tone.

★ Learn the lesson. Try and work out what caused the injury and address it. For lower leg issues (i.e. knee / ankle), a trip to a podiatrist may uncover a biomechanical cause. You may need different running shoes, or to be careful with certain movements. You may also need to strengthen up the area to help prevent it recurring.

★ Increase intensity slowly. It's likely you will not be as fit as you were before the injury. Keep this in mind and slowly increase distances and intensity. You may also need extra rest days.

# AUGUST

If July is holiday month, then August is Edinburgh festival month. If you're a festival addict, check out the article on staying healthy over the festival month.

## WHAT'S IN SEASON

It's peak growing season in Scotland, so enjoy:

**Artichoke, aubergine, beetroot, broad beans, broccoli, carrots, courgettes, cucumber, fennel, french beans, garlic, kohlrabi, mangetout, marrows, new potatoes, onions, peas, potatoes, radishes, rocket, runner beans, sorrel, spring onions, turnips, watercress, apricots, blackberries, blueberries, cherries, gooseberries, loganberries, melons, radishes, raspberries, redcurrants, strawberries, tomatoes.**

## OATCAKE TOPPING OF THE MONTH

Cottage cheese and peaches: a truly delicious combination for summer.

# Easy Summer Recipes

## Gazpacho Soup

*One of my husband Andy's favourite dishes, this authentic Spanish cold soup is refreshing in hot weather.*

*Serves 6 (good to eat the next day too, if you have leftovers)*

1 red onion, finely chopped
3 tomatoes, finely chopped
½ medium cucumber, finely diced
½ green pepper, seeded and finely chopped
½ red pepper, seeded and finely chopped
1 clove garlic, crushed
3½ cups (875ml) tomato juice
½ tsp sugar
Salt and freshly ground pepper
3 tbsp olive oil
3 tbsp white wine vinegar

★ Mix all together in a big bowl and refrigerate.
★ Serve with optional croutons. To make croutons, trim crusts from some bread and cut into 1cm cubes. Bake in an oven, drizzled with a tiny amount of olive oil (you can use garlic oil for flavour) until golden.

## Atenjene Raheb – Lebanese Aubergine and Tomato Salad

*This easy salad is great for lunch with pita bread, or as an accompaniment to dinner.*

*Serves two or four as an accompaniment*

2 medium aubergines
2 medium ripe tomatoes, diced
1 red onion, finely chopped
½ lemon, juiced
1 tbsp olive oil
1 clove garlic, crushed: fresh or roasted garlic or a drizzle of garlic oil
6 leaves fresh mint
Small handful of fresh parsley (a generous shake of dried parsley is OK).
Sea salt and freshly ground pepper

* Roast the aubergines in a 220°C oven until soft.
* Cool, then peel skin off.
* Chop the flesh and gently mash in with lemon juice, olive oil, garlic, mint, parsley, salt and pepper.
* Spread the puree on a serving plate and sprinkle with chopped tomato and red onion.
* Dip into with triangles of toasted wholemeal pita bread and enjoy.

## Fennel and Tomato Bake

*If gazpacho is my husband's favourite summer dish, then this is mine.*

One large fennel (or two small)
200 – 250g cherry tomatoes
Splash olive oil
Juice of half a lemon
Sea salt and cracked pepper
Few springs of fresh thyme
Tiny wee splash balsamic vinegar (optional)

* Wash and remove the tough outer bits of the fennel, and chop the base out in a 'V' shape.
* Cut into 5mm slices, then steam until nearly tender.
* Wash the cherry tomatoes and combine with the steamed fennel in a casserole dish.
* Drizzle over olive oil, balsamic and lemon juice, add salt, pepper and thyme (fresh parsley tastes yummy too).
* Toss it all to combine and cook on a high shelf in an oven at about 220°C.
* Cook for about 20 minutes or until the tomatoes are bursting from their skin.
* Serve hot or allow to cool to room temperature.

## Ratatouille

Ratatouille is a very versatile Provençal dish that is traditionally served with meat. I like it on top of steamed new potatoes or with veggie burgers. This recipe makes a big pot, and it keeps well in the fridge or freezer. I don't worry too much about how much olive oil is in it, as it makes such a big pot that lasts for ages. Also, it's definitely more nutritious than shop-bought sauces. All ingredients are approximate as traditionally it was made to use up old vegetables. Keeping the lid on the pot whenever possible will ensure the success of this recipe.

* Slice five large shallots or two large onions into long strips.
* Finely chop 8 cloves of garlic, or even more if you like.
* Heat about ¼ cup of olive oil in a large, preferably heavy bottomed pot and soften shallots / onion on a medium heat. Put the lid on the pot.
* Add the garlic, stir and keep the lid on.
* Cube 1 – 2 aubergines and add to the pot to brown.
* Chop 2 – 4 courgettes into chunks. Add to the pot and stir gently.
* If you're running out of oil in the pot, add a little more oil or some water.
* Chop up any old tomatoes you have hanging around. Don't bother with them if they are hard. Add to the pot.
* Toss in 1 –2 tins of tomatoes. Use your judgement about how tomato-ey you'd like it. You can also use passata.
* Season well. Twist pepper grinder a good dozen times and added a wee bit of sea salt. If you are using dried herbs, add them now. I tossed in a handful of herbs d'Provence (mixed herbs). You can use dried basil, rosemary,

marjoram, oregano, mint – don't be shy. If you're using fresh herbs, toss them in towards the end.

★ You will notice bubbles of olive oil on the top. This is good. Reduce the heat to the lowest setting on the smallest ring you have. Even better, use a hotpot.

★ The idea is to keep the pot on the lowest heat as possible for at least an hour. Try not to stir it too much and definitely leave the lid on. If it's bubbling it's too hot.

★ Even better, leave it in the pot off the heat for a few hours. The latent heat will keep it cooking.

★ You can add the fresh herbs just before you are ready to serve.

## Stuffed Marrow

*Serves four*

*You can't get more seasonal than a giant marrow straight from an allotment. There is a knack to carving the marrow whilst leaving it whole, so get the big knives out.*

A marrow
100g rice
1 stock cube or fresh stock
1 red pepper
1 small onion, finely chopped
2 cloves garlic, finely chopped
6 mushrooms
1 small carrot
Handful of parsley or your favourite herbs
½ tsp cumin
1 tbsp olive oil
Ground pepper to taste (no need for salt as it has stock in it)

★ Preheat oven to 200°C. Wash and cut the ends off the marrow.

★ Scoop out the seeds from the middle of the marrow using a spoon to create a marrow 'tube'. Retain the ends for later use and compost the scooped mush. If this is too challenging, you can simply scoop out the marrow that has been halved lengthwise.

★ Cook rice in water with a small amount of stock for flavour.

* Chop the vegetables and herbs finely. You can use other vegetables if you wish.
* Sauté onion and garlic in olive oil. When softened add the other vegetables, cumin and black pepper and cook with the lid on. You can add a bit of water if it starts to stick.
* When cooked, stir in the rice.
* Hold marrow upright for stuffing, with one of the ends held over the bottom hole so the stuffing doesn't fall out. When you've stuffed it from one end, turn it upside down and stuff the other end.
* Or if you've gone for the easy option simply fill halved and scooped marrow.
* Place in a baking tray in the oven for 45 minutes (or more depending on size of marrow).
* Serve in slices.

# Resisting Temptation Hints of the Month

## Get a Snacking Bowl

Eating small meals regularly throughout the day is a proven way to boost your metabolism. However some people are afraid to snack in case they eat too much. A simple solution is to purchase a snacking bowl. Invest in a bowl that is small in size, a sauce-dipping bowl from a Chinese supermarket is ideal. Find yourself a really nice looking bowl that you will enjoy using. Even a ramekin will suffice. Never eat straight from a packet or container, always measure your snack into a small bowl, put the packet away and then commence nibbling. And choose healthy options like dried fruit, nuts, chopped raw vegetables (i.e. peppers or carrots), grapes or seeds. Obviously.

## Go Slow

As frustrating as it may be, try using chopsticks when you're in an Asian restaurant. It will slow down how fast you shovel food into your mouth and also assist your coordination.

## Beware the Exercise Appetite

It's wonderful when you start exercising as your appetite increases. However there's no need to go overboard with it. If you're aiming to lose weight, you need to burn more calories than you're ingesting so you can burn your fat stores. For instance, if you reward yourself for a half hour brisk walk to work with a digestive biscuit, you may as well catch the bus and not bother with the biscuit. So when peckish from exercising, be very aware of exactly what you're snacking on…

# Fad or Fab

## Power Plate

For the uninitiated a Power Plate is a vibrating platform that you stand and exercise on. The theory is that the vibrations temporarily put your body off balance, so you engage more muscles just by maintaining your position. It's a very vibrationary experience. It can tone your muscles pronto although the downside is that intense vibrations can be somewhat disconcerting.

Personally I prefer a quieter workout and am happy to spend a bit more time on exercise I enjoy. For those who are strapped for time or enjoy being jiggled, then this may help you. This technology is here to stay.

## Simple is Best

This gadget is simple – it's a digital egg timer. "How does this get you fit?" you may well ask. Just ask anyone who's done a Griffen Fitness egg timer circuit session. Instead of sets and reps, mix things up by doing strength exercises by the minute. A minute of press-ups may not sound much, but it's amazing how many reps you can fit in whilst exercising against the clock. It's also amazing how many exercises you can fit into a timed ten minutes. Surely you have ten minutes in your day to do some exercise?

## Air and Water

Air and water are two basic necessities of life. It's not surprising there's a load of products out there around this theme. Firstly I'll look at hydration and the newly evolved Camelbak. Camelbak is a 'hydration system' in a backpack. Basically it's a backpack full of water (in a plastic bladder). The plastic tube you stick in your mouth looks a bit medical, however it's a godsend for long bike rides, runs or hill walks.

Also on the hydration theme is the Brita filter jug, which I love. Edinburgh water is really very good compared to London water, but still there is a slight residual taste of chlorine. A filter jug removes this odour and also any nasty heavy metals that we shouldn't drink. It also means you can keep a jug of water at room temperature, an ideal temperature for suppng. Two fabulous hydration innovations.

Moving swiftly onto air, I tried two 'oxygen supplements'. I felt a bit of a dipstick paying for air, but in the name of research I tried Oxyshots, containing "CSO2™ Charged Stabilised Oxygen – a literally space-age technology pioneered by NASA and produced exclusively from natural ingredients." In plain English it was 10mL saline solution with a saturation of oxygen. For £1.60 I bought 10mL of salty water. Ho hum.

Wandering through Harvey Nichols I was intrigued by another oxygen product called 'Big Ox'. For £6 I could have purchased a (very light) pressurized container of flavoured air. Being a canny shopper I waited for the sales, when loads and loads of the cans were on sale for £2 each. Upon reflection I was still ripped off, even though it came in a nice tin. So don't be an oxymoron – if you want more oxygen, just breathe a little deeper.

## Exercise of the Month: Posture Check

As you read this, do a posture check. Are you slumped down in your chair, belly sticking out? Sit up tall with your tummy in. By engaging your abdominal muscles (i.e. holding them in), you exercise them and promote better posture. Our sedentary lifestyles encourage belly bulge, so we need to consciously combat 'slouch pouch'.

If you have Outlook as your email programme, set a regular calendar reminder to check your posture. For those of you without the presence of a Microsoft reminder, set an alarm to go off throughout the day to remind you. See if you can maintain good posture for five minutes, and gradually build it up. Imagine you are walking into a room of people who you'd like to impress and take that as your posture benchmark. After practise, you will find that you automatically remind yourself to correct slumping.

# August Articles

## Festival Fitness

It's that crazy time of year in auld reekie when common sense is abandoned for the pursuit of all things hedonistic – yes, it's festival month.

If you're an Edinburgh resident, you will have seen it all before and may have even been to the Penny Black pub at 5am. For those of you who are Festival virgins, here is a brief guide to damage control:

★ Be sure to have some yummy breakfast food purchased and ready to go. It really is the most important meal of the day energy-wise.

★ Carry a bottle of water around with you at all times. You'll get so sick of carrying it that it will force you to drink it. Also some Festival venues are notoriously hot. I remember a very stuffy comedy show where the comedian encouraged the audience to take off their tops to cool down. Avoid embarrassment and keep your cool.

★ Carry a small bag of nuts and seeds with you. Handy for nibbling on at a show or when you're queuing to get in. Oatcakes and raw food bars are also handy snacks on the go.

★ Walk! Walking between venues is the quickest way to get around town when it's suffering festival congestion.

★ Get some perspective: wander up Calton Hill, Arthur's Seat, or for a cracking view of the Old Town, Salisbury Crags.

★ Just say 'no'. Not only to the multitude of flyers thrust upon you on the Royal Mile, but no to the 'just one more drink'.

★ If you didn't say no the night before, a good Vitamin B complex supplement can take the edge off and also helps replace booze depleted vitamins.

★ Work out how much sleep you need (especially if you're holding down a fulltime non festival job) and work backwards. Do you really need to go to that cabaret act at midnight on a Wednesday? Your immune system will thank you for sleeping more.

# Be Buoyant! Diving Into Water for Exercise

It's great to get wet… it's one of my favourite forms of exercise and boy, does it burn up those calories. I'm talking about jumping into a swimming pool of course.

You can move in so many ways that are not possible on land. With fluidity and without effort, movement in water has fitness benefits for all ages. Water provides a supportive resistance, which makes it the number one training medium for anyone with dodgy knees, creaky limbs, balance issues, a baby on the way or an uncomfortable amount of body fat (fat is buoyant, so it's a bonus in the water). It's refreshing so you don't even notice when you're sweating.

So with that glowing introduction, I bet you're wondering exactly what you can do in water if you're a non-swimmer. There are two options, either learn to swim or work with what you've got. It's not essential to be a swimmer to benefit from being in the water. Hydrotherapy, rehabilitation in water, is used by some medical professionals and involves exercises like walking in the water – which helps posture and strengthens your 'core' muscles. There are many other exercises that can help strengthen stabilising muscles around dodgy knees without worsening the injury. In fact, many professional sport players use aqua exercise for rehabilitation or as an alternative method of resistance training. A friend with MS finds moving in water much easier than moving on land.

One idea is to attend a local aqua aerobics class. Classes during the day tend to attract the blue-hair brigade (who are great fun to exercise with, but do little for your workout ego), so go to an evening class if you'd like to be pushed a little harder. Try and memorise as many exercises as you can and then you can replicate them at will, when you are having a swim session yourself, or even on holiday.

# The Art of Running

Running is one of the simplest and most effective exercises the human body can do. Not only do we strengthen our heart, muscles and bones, we can also use the time running to leave our worries behind, solve problems and feel good about ourselves. To get started, all you need is the will to move.

## Equipment

Shoes are obviously a necessity, but which ones? A good quality pair of trainers need not cost the earth. There's a new-fangled belief that everyone should go to a running specialist shop. If you're starting out running, it's unlikely you'll be running marathons. Unless you have flat feet, suffer from any foot discomfort or your shoes wear out unevenly, a standard pair of running shoes should suffice.

For women, a good sports bra is an absolute necessity. You want a good fitting to ensure your assets stay in good shape as you shape up. Get properly fitted and you'll be much more comfortable.

Also essential is a fast-wicking T-shirt that will draw moisture away from the body. For cold winter nights, high visibility clothing is useful.

## The run:

★ Give yourself 30 minutes to an hour after eating before setting out or you may have a gurgling tummy or the dreaded 'stitch'. Be sure to hydrate before you start.

★ Check a map and set a route before you leave. Start small, perhaps a lap around the park, and build up with time.

★ If you're running alone, let someone know where you're heading.

★ Set off slower than you think you'd like to run. It's good to warm up, and you can always increase the pace when you've settled into your stride. Many new folk start off at breakneck speed and exhaust themselves quickly, putting themselves off running by trying to achieve too much too soon.

★ If you find yourself tiring and not able to continue, drop down to a fast walk (don't stop). Tell yourself "I am going to walk to the next light pole / bench / intersection and then set back off again". What you will be effectively doing is interval training (described on page 84). Make the intervals smaller (i.e. run more and walk less) next time you're out. Alternatively you can adjust the pace so you can run the whole distance without stopping.

★ If you do the same route over and over again, within the space of a few runs, you will find the whole thing a lot easier.

★ When you master your starting route, give yourself a pat on the back, before altering the route. It is important to recognise training landmarks: did the route seem impossible to begin with? One of the best things about running is the sense of achievement you get from completing a route. It's always entertaining to try your usual route backwards.

★ After you have mastered the concept of going out for a run, start timing yourself. Having a time to beat is a great incentive to get out there. You can also time how long it takes you to do half your run, so that you know whether you are up to speed halfway through your run. If your first half is slower than usual, you can make up time on the way home.

★ Some people find having a goal to work towards a good incentive. There are all sorts of charity runs around that you can enter (and make money for a good cause). If you're unsure about entering a large run, try walking it for the first year and running the following summer.

★ Take your portable music device out with you with an inspirational soundtrack. Try Bruce Springsteen's *Born to Run*, Soul to Soul's *Keep on Moving* and the soundtrack to *Chariots of Fire* (for the slow-motion sprint home).

★ Always give yourself 10 minutes or so to cool down and stretch after every single run. No excuses. Hold stretches for at least 30 seconds to increase flexibility and don't bounce. Stretching will help prevent stiff muscles and also give you something to look forward to at the end of each run.

★ Log your run. Writing down your runs (distance, time and route) will give you structure to your running programme, and incentives to develop.

★ Give yourself a day to recover between runs, especially when starting out.

As we are all built differently, we all have our own running style. However there are some pointers to look out for whilst developing your own style. Starting from the top down:

Keep your shoulders and neck relaxed at all times, leave your tension behind you. When swinging your arms, keep elbows at ninety degrees and hands moving forward, to propel yourself forward. Many people run crossing their arms across their bodies, rather than pushing forward. If you think about balance, by crossing the direction of arm swing over the mid line they move their weight from side to side, rather than forwards.

Abdominals should always be engaged to help protect the back and keep upright. Feet need to be picked up, avoiding the 'soft shoe shuffle'. Not only will this move you faster, but will help you from tripping over. It may sound obvious, but it is easy to let feet drag on the ground. Replacing your trainers regularly (once a year for occasional runners, every six months for regular pavement pounders) will help keep the spring in your step. A word about bounce, don't overdo it. What you're looking for is a nice smooth style without too much up and down. In a similar fashion to criss crossing arms wasting energy, jiggling up and down also wastes energy in the vertical plane. The thing to remember is that you would like to move forward horizontally in as smooth a style as possible. A visualisation that I find useful is imagining myself moving along one of the moving footways that are found in airports. Smoooooth.

# And importantly... Breathing

As your body undertakes more strenuous exercise, your muscles require more oxygen. Unfortunately many of us either forget to breathe more, or haven't trained our lungs sufficiently to get enough oxygen in. It's easy to get stressed out when in this state and start gasping for breath. This is the last thing we should do, as panicking is counter-productive to deep breathing. My solution is to do breathing exercises separately from running. If you think about it, running = legs + breathing. Large muscle groups moving at speed require an increased intake of oxygen. So to train the body to breathe properly, let me take you through an adaptation of a Zen breathing exercise Jonathon Clogstoun-Wilmott, an Edinburgh acupuncturist, taught me. This was originally given to me for relaxation, but I have found it works brilliantly for running:

1.  Sit yourself down somewhere quiet for a few minutes where you will not be disturbed.

2.  Ensure your limbs are uncrossed and you are comfortable.

3.  Lightly close your eyes, or let them relax and go out of focus.

4.  Concentrate entirely on your breathing. Breathe in deeply and slowly through your nose, filling your lungs bit by bit until they are completely full of air. As you breathe in, focus on the number one appearing. Do not let your concentration wander.

5.  Slowly exhale through your mouth as you imagine the number one disappearing. Completely empty your lungs, but stay relaxed.

6.  Repeat inhalation through nose, visualising the number two. Be conscious of only your breath and the number two, as your lungs fully inflate.

7.  Exhale slowly through your mouth imaging the number two fading.

8.  Repeat up to ten.

By practising breathing in such a fashion, you promote a deep sense of relaxation and encourage your body to take in more oxygen. It may take a bit of practise to get into the relaxed state (distractions in modern life abound), but when you have got the hang of it, you can return to that relaxed state when you are running. If you find yourself out of breath, try returning mentally to that relaxed state and slowing down your breathing and opening up your chest. Even if you don't get a chance to try this exercise (not enough time to breathe anyone?), think about the concept of deep breathing next time you are out running. Very relaxing.

# Functional Fitness, Everyday Fitness

Historically the role of a personal trainer has focussed on sports specific training, that is, training athletes and sports people to be fitter and stronger specifically for their sport. Footballers may have had a coach to motivate them and teach them tactics and a PT to take them to the gym to ensure they're fit for the game. Over the last 20 or so years there has been a huge shift in a PT's every day role. You find personal trainers in public gyms, training outdoors, working from private studios and even going to clients' houses. Now, not all these clients are athletes, and not all these people are already fit.

The majority of my clients are everyday folk who would simply like to be a bit fitter, trimmer and have more energy in their day to day life. Functional fitness encompasses exercises to help you function better in life. Doing a squat is like sitting down in a chair, a dumbbell row is like sawing a piece of wood, lunges work your hill walking muscles at the front of your thigh (quads), an upright row like lifting a backpack onto your back.

Many traditional gym programmes focus on the muscles that you can see in the mirror (chest, abs and the front of the body). This is all very well if you want to pose in your underwear, but if you're interested in remaining injury free in everyday life, you need to remember to work the muscles that you can't see equally to keep your back safe when you're lifting and carrying. Rather than using machine weights that tend to isolate muscle groups, try body weight and dumbbell exercises that encourage muscle groups to work together. Your 'form' (posture) when you practise pulling and heaving movements needs to be precise, so it is often helpful to have someone else training with you (fitness trainer or a 'spotter').

# SEPTEMBER

September is an unlikely month in Edinburgh. Although the days are getting shorter, the weather can be rather mild. An Indian summer of unexpected sunny days is perfect for exercising outdoors.

## WHAT'S IN SEASON

Artichoke, aubergine, beetroot, broad beans, broccoli, carrots, courgettes, cucumber, fennel, french beans, garlic, kohlrabi, mangetout, onions, peas, potatoes (maincrop), radishes, rocket, runner beans, sorrel, turnips, watercress, apricots, blackberries, blueberries, cherries, gooseberries, loganberries, melons, radishes, raspberries, redcurrants, strawberries, tomatoes.

## OATCAKE TOPPING OF THE MONTH

For something different, try olive tapenade with a slice of feta on your oatcake. Add a slice of tomato for extra colour and juiciness. How Mediterranean! You can make tapenade easily at home. Simply blend kalamata olives in a food processor with a squeeze of lemon juice and some capers.

# Easy Autumn Recipes

## Dairy Banana Smoothie

The milk, yoghurt and wheatgerm in this smoothie makes it a slow burning energy drink (also a good source of calcium to maintain strong bones). The thick texture is quite filling. The minus side is that some people might find the amount of dairy quite cloying (you can use rice, soy or oat milk instead).

Blend:

1 – 2 bananas (the older the better, it's a good way to use manky black bananas)
Large dollop of natural / flavoured yoghurt
A cup of semi skimmed milk
Squeeze of honey (optional)
1 tbsp wheatgerm or sunflower seeds (optional)

## Easy Fruity Smoothie

This is a fruity fix of vitamins.

Blend:

1 banana
handful of strawberries
¼ melon
a cup of orange juice
squeeze of lime / lemon juice

## Go Troppo! Smoothie

Instead of using acidic orange juice as a base for the smoothie, use a middle of the road juice like guava or mango to make a delicious tropical smoothie.

Blend:

1 banana (of course)
Handful of berries, melon and / or some ripe pineapple
A dollop of yoghurt is optional, and turns it into a lassi
1 cup of guava or mango juice

## Bollywood Smoothie

So named as it has a light and frothy Indian flavour

Blend:

  1 banana
  200 ml pineapple juice
  2 ice cubes
  1 mint ice cube or a few fresh mint leaves.
  1 tbsp natural yoghurt

## Bruschetta

Lovely ripe tomatoes are still in season, and now is the best time of year to eat fancy tomatoes on toast a.k.a bruschetta. Tomatoes are packed full of vitamins and antioxidants, including Lycopene (which is meant to have protective qualities against some cancers). This simple recipe is really tasty for a snack or starter. Be sure to use tomatoes at room temperature, which have more flavour than refrigerated.

  One unsliced loaf of proper bread, experiment to find your favourite
  Ripe tomatoes, I use ½ a tomato per slice
  Handful of basil, ripped
  Good quality olive oil
  Ground black pepper
  Clove of garlic, halved

★ Slice the bread medium thickness and brush both sides of each slice with olive oil.
★ Finely dice the tomatoes and mix in basil and black pepper.
★ Lightly grill both sides of bread then rub each side with half a clove of garlic.
★ Heap the topping on each slice just prior to serving.

# Colourful Summer Salad

This is a flavoursome high fibre treat. Get good quality vegetables from a greengrocer rather than the supermarket, and you will taste a noticeable difference.

*Serves four as a side salad*

½ kohlrabi, peeled and grated
1 carrot, grated
4 radishes, finely sliced
½ red onion, finely chopped
½ red pepper, finely chopped
Handful chopped coriander
2 tsp sesame oil
4 tsp white wine or rice vinegar
4 tsp light soy sauce

★ Combine all of the above in a salad bowl and enjoy.

# Herby Potato Salad

*...A healthy alternative*

500g potatoes (waxy or new)
250g natural yoghurt
½ lemon, juiced
Handful of mixed chopped herbs (parsley, rosemary, mint, dill or your favourite)
Ground pepper

★ Wash, then chop the potatoes into chunks and boil until tender. I like to leave the skin on for extra taste and nutrition, but peel if you must.
★ Drain and rinse under cold water to stop the potatoes cooking and going soggy.
★ Mix remaining ingredients in a bowl and toss in the cooled potato chunks.
★ This keeps OK in the fridge for a day, so is good to take for lunch.

# Resisting Temptation Hints of the Month

## Be Like A Bison

Have you ever noticed on wildlife documentaries how animals, including bison, flock around water? Humans are very clever animals indeed and in the Western world don't need to flock to water supplies – we even have it coming into our homes. Aren't we lucky? So why don't we drink enough of the stuff?

Be clever and create 'lagoons' of water so you will always have something to drink. Whether at work or at home, always have a glass of water to hand to sup on. If it's in front of you, you're more likely to drink it. Also take a glass of water to bed with you.

## Don't Buy Rubbish Food

If you need to visit to a supermarket, make a shopping list and stick to it.

Walk straight past the crisp and biscuit aisle.

Resist the 2-4-1 offers on snack food that you didn't even plan on buying.

Notice they rarely have healthy 2-4-1 offers.

# Fad or Fab

## Blisters No More

Do you get blisters when running? I do, especially if my feet are hot at the end of a long run. I thought I had tried everything, including meths on the feet, Compeed and blister-preventing socks. All of which had little effect. Imagine my joy when Rat Race team mate Ian introduced me to the simple solution of zinc oxide tape. It's basically an easy-tear adhesive tape that you can strap any problem spots with. It is very gentle to tender skin and prevents rubbing. You can pick up a roll from the internet or any good running shop for a couple of quid. Truly fabulous.

## Rubber Resistance

Most people imagine resistance work as weight training in the gym – lifting heavy weights and bulking up. In fact, we all should do some resistance work to strengthen our muscles and joints, but not everyone likes working with metal weights. Try using rubber.

Resistance tubes and bands offer a great option for toning up but not bulking up. Any exercise you can do in a gym, you can do at home with rubber resistance.

## Exercise of the Month: Stair Climbing

Try walking up stairs two at a time. Even better if you have short legs, with a bit of practise you will increase your leg strength and flexibility. Specifically it targets your quadriceps (front of thigh), hamstrings (back of thigh) and gluteus maximus (rear end). You'll really notice the difference in your leg strength.

# September Articles

## It's all about Rhythm

Exercise and music are made for each other – they go hand in hand and have always done. Why is this?

Music encourages people to work harder, especially when it's their choice of tunes. I had one home visit client who always used to row the same distance (somewhat reluctantly) as a warm up. One morning I insisted he put on some of his favourite music through his lounge room sound system. His rowing speed increased by at least 10%, just because he "forgot that I was rowing as I was enjoying the song so much." That kind of statement is gold dust to a personal trainer, and I view good music as an integral part of any workout. A close friend of mine agrees that she has improved her run time simply by popping on some headphones.

If you break it down and think of the structure of music as a series of rhythmical beats, it starts to make sense. The idea of listening to a beat that mimics the tempo of what you're doing ensures that speed is maintained, and almost as importantly, that you're in an 'up' mood… or relaxed if you're listening to mellow chill out music when stretching.

There are times where music can be distracting, for instance if learning a new movement, or when it's so loud it's dangerous (think of cyclists or joggers oblivious to the outside world with headphones on). Also sometimes it's nice to listen to the world around you. However it's fair to say that the right choice of music can motivate you to push yourself further than you're used to.

So you don't need to prance about in lycra and leg warmers to appreciate the power that music can give your workout. Get funky!

# Location, Location, Location: The Great Outdoors Vs Gym Indoors

Exercise is evolving. Now, more than ever, we have a wide variety of options of how to stay in shape. Here's a comparison of exercising in a gym versus 'anywhere else':

## Gym Environment

★ It doesn't matter what the weather is like outdoors, you will always be warm and dry. But what if it's sunny?

★ You can always watch television whilst pounding away on the treadmill.

★ Many gyms have motivational music… but do you like pumping techno?

★ In most gyms you will have an expansive choice of up-to-date equipment.

★ There's often one inconsiderate gym user who never wipes down his sweaty bench. Not nice.

★ You may feel motivated by all of the other folk around you. Aerobics classes are a great way to use other folk to motivate you.

★ Negotiating bunches of burly blokes in the weights area and queueing for machines can be off-putting.

★ Some like to use the gym to search for potential mates (in every sense of the word).

★ Swimming pools, jacuzzis, saunas and steam rooms make all the hard work worthwhile.

★ It's great to have different elements to your workout. Some people like to do weights some days, classes on other days and perfecting their swimming stroke as an additional element to their workouts.

★ A gym membership can be handy for cold winter weather.

★ All of the cardio machines measure distance and your heart rate, which is important for tracking progress.

★ Not all gyms are adequately staffed which can be an injury risk.

## Anywhere Else

* It's great to get outdoors, and it has been proven beneficial to spend a bit of each day somewhere green. Seasonal Affective Disorder may be helped if you spend a bit of time outdoors each day, no matter the weather.

* Running outdoors is more challenging than running on a treadmill. A treadmill moves under your feet and you effectively jog on the spot. When you get outdoors you have both propulsion and the natural elements to contend with. Running on different surfaces (i.e. grass, dirt tracks) also strengthens stabilising muscles in your ankles and legs.

* Fresh air.

* Commuting to work by bike or on foot is an easy way to get your baseline cardio work in regularly.

* Try hill walking on the weekend, or discover a new route around where you live.

* If you're exercising in the home, you can choose your own music and television shows.

* You can also choose what time of day you work out, and have more flexibility timewise to your work outs.

* If you're exercising from home you are unlikely to have the full range of equipment that a traditional gym offers. Sometimes storage is an issue, especially if you're lifting heavy weights.

* In tenement flats noise is also an issue. For example, a treadmill in a flat may not be appropriate.

* If you have children, it is important that they see you exercising. Get them involved too. A family bike ride, or walk along the beach will teach your kids that exercise is an important part of everyday life.

# Creatures of Habit

Are you creature of habit? The definition of a habit is interesting, "an acquired behaviour pattern regularly followed until it has become almost involuntary"

As humans we are largely intelligent beings. Using our intelligence, we work out patterns of behaviour that make our lives easier. For instance, we can work out the quickest way to get ready for work in the morning. The easiest way to drive to work. Our favourite seat on the bus. The best place to buy our lunch, and the fastest way to get there. And so on, until the end of the day, when we always brush our teeth before bed and sleep on the same side of bed each night.

On the whole this is largely a good thing. It means we are able to achieve a lot with minimum effort.

However, when it comes to getting fit, being a creature of habit is not necessarily the way to be. Minimum effort equals minimum calories burnt. To get fit, we need to make our lives a bit more difficult, we need to expend more energy, we need to break our habits.

Where to start? Firstly it's important to identify your habits. Do you always walk the same way to the bus stop? Do you use you car for short journeys? Do you always have a glass of wine when you're cooking dinner? Or always go to the pub after work on a Friday? Do you always buy the same brand of cereal?

Changing habits can seem painful at the time, but think about how quickly you learnt the habit. Sometimes it's a matter of slipping. For instance, sleeping in a bit later each morning, so eventually you don't even have time for breakfast. Just by getting up 15 minutes earlier you can change your whole morning. Instead of jumping out of bed, into the shower and racing to work, you can relax and enjoy a good breakfast, setting you up for the day and helping you feel more prepared. You may even start to enjoy your mornings.

If you work in an office, do you email people who are in the same room as you? Get up, go over to them and tell them what you were going to type. Obviously there are exceptions to this, but if you start thinking "outside the box" and replacing some of your "time-saving" habits (I put this in quotations, as quite often these methods aren't time saving at all) with something more old-fashioned, you'll be burning more calories.

Fitness-wise, it's not uncommon for people to 'cheat' on exercises. Cheating on an exercise in fitness terms means losing form to complete an exercise. This losing form makes the exercise easier to complete and uses less effort. This is a similar idea to habits, as it is a human's natural intelligence looking for the easy way to do something.

Becoming fit is not about how easy something is, it's about enjoying the challenge and training your body to cope with it.

## Reach Your Goals with a Food Diary

If you aim to change your eating habits, a food diary is a very powerful tool. Writing down exactly what you eat, how much and when will give you a good idea of your eating habits. A food diary is useful on many levels:

★ It makes you accountable, so you think twice before popping that chocolate in your mouth.
★ It highlights existing habits i.e. snacking in the evening.
★ Including writing down everything you drink can also help you drink more water (one of the most basic aspects of good health is hydration).
★ It can help track peaks and troughs in energy levels, especially if you are a caffeine / chocolate fiend.

A food diary is a time commitment and you need to ensure it is updated regularly and thoroughly for it to be meaningful. Remember to write down absolutely everything (this includes if you have a bite of someone's sandwich, or finish off your children's food). Weighing some of your basic foods is also a useful exercise (also to ensure your portions are actually standard size). Knowing the quantity that you eat is crucial if you use an online tool like the very fine (and free) www.foodfocus.co.uk. An online food diary will also show you the nutritional content of your food. The quality of information you receive online is only as accurate what you input, so it's useful to keep labels of food for the nutritional content. Even better, eat food with no labels.

There are a number of limiting factors with a food diary. It is common for people to forget about snacks (indeed, I once met a person who snacked at midnight, but did not recall until I picked up on it through conversation). Or, the situation where a packet of biscuits is opened and the amount consumed underestimated. I have found that many people feel guilty about situations like this and find writing it down almost an impossible task. If you make yourself accountable, it is likely that you will be more mindful of how much of the packet is consumed.

We all like treats, and a food diary will show you if you're indulging in treats as a regular habit, or indeed as a treat.

Eating can be wrapped up in emotional issues, so if you feel unsure about a food diary, just try it for a day. Carry it around with you so you remember to write in it. Remember it is natural to slip up, and that you can still enjoy going out for dinner and occasional indulgences. A food diary should highlight that your average day-to-day habits are healthy. Check you're getting your five servings of fruit and vegetables a day, that you are prioritising wholegrain over white carbs and that you are drinking enough water and you will be well on the way to good health.

# OCTOBER

Yes, it's October, the time of carving pumpkins, shorter days and rugging up. It's also the time of year when shops start advertising Christmas, but we can ignore that until December...

## WHAT'S IN SEASON

**Apples, beetroot, blackberries, butternut squash, courgettes, damsons, elderberries, figs, kale, land cress, marrow, mushrooms, pears, plums, potatoes (main crop), pumpkin, radishes, rocket, samphire (found beside the sea), sweetcorn, watercress.**

## OATCAKE TOPPING OF THE MONTH

Like cheese? Then you need to try Crowdie, a Scottish cheese that's low in fat and literally made for oatcakes. Crowdie is one of the world's oldest cheeses originating from the Highlands. It was thought that this soft cheese on oatcakes counteracted the affects of whisky, and was a traditional snack before going to a Ceilidh. I like it because it's only 4.5% fat, has a yummy tangy flavour and goes with almost any other oatcake topping.

# Easy Autumn Recipes

## Ginger Beer

*This ginger beer recipe is really rather refreshing. It's a great post-exercise treat, or if you're feeling a little run down.*

Ginger has anti-inflammatory properties and is also good for tummy problems (ginger can be used for motion sickness amongst other things). Indian Ayurvedic medicine uses ginger for its warming properties. Ginger can be eaten and can also be used externally, in massage oils and baths, to help restore balance to the system. It's a good reason to try the below (very easy) method to make ginger beer.

2 litre bottle of still mineral water*
Large chunk of root ginger, the best value and freshest is from an Indian supermarket. Don't buy wrinkly stuff.
1 lemon
1 cup of sugar, for this recipe white is best
¼ tsp of dried yeast, you can buy it in small sachets for bread making

\* You can either use store-bought bottled water or tap water. I have a water filter jug, so I use this. You can use any 2 litre PET bottle that has had fizzy drink in.

★ Decant the water into a suitable temporary container (skip this step if you are using tap / filter jug water)

★ Using a plastic funnel, pour the sugar into the bottle.

★ Add the dried yeast to the bottle.

★ Grate the ginger until you have about 2 tablespoon's worth. Feel free to vary this according to your taste. Shove into bottle.

★ Next, extract the juice from one lemon and add to bottle.

★ Now you need to add the water to the bottle. Fill until there is approximately a one inch gap at the top, then put the cap on and shake the bottle until all the sugar is dissolved.

★ Screw the cap on the bottle as tightly as you can, then place the bottle somewhere warm for about 48 hours to let the yeast go to work. Once the bottle is very hard and can't be squeezed, the ginger beer is done.

- ★ Place the bottle in the fridge overnight. This halts the yeast and stops the bottle exploding.
- ★ Strain and enjoy.

## Land Cress Soup

Land cress is also known as Belle Isle cress, early yellowrocket, American cress, American watercress, dryland cress, upland cress, cassabully, creasy salad or early winter cress. It flourishes in our allotment, and seems resistant to slugs. It looks a bit like watercress (but on land) with lovely crinkly leaves that are easy to harvest and useful in the kitchen. This recipe also contains leeks and potatoes that grow well in bonnie Scotland.

*Serves four*

1 leek
250g potatoes, skins on, more or less to taste
1 tbsp olive oil
200g washed land cress, or watercress
750ml vegetable stock
Dollop natural yoghurt to serve

- ★ Chop leeks and potatoes into smallish bits. It will get blended later so don't worry about consistent shapes.
- ★ Sauté leeks in a little oil, add potatoes and stir to coat and cook a bit.
- ★ Add the vegetable stock and stir in. Cook with lid on for about 20 minutes until the potatoes are soft.
- ★ Add washed cress and cook on low heat with lid on for another 10 minutes.
- ★ Zizz with a hand blender until smooth and a healthy shade of green. You can add some more water and heat through if you prefer a thin soup.
- ★ Season with lots of fresh ground black pepper and serve with a dollop of natural yoghurt.

## Playing with Polenta

*Polenta, bright yellow cornmeal, is a quick and easy gluten-free alternative to pasta and wheat-based pizza bases.*

For 4 servings pour 250g dry polenta into a jug. Heat 1 litre of water in a heavy bottom pan until boiling. When at a rolling boil, slowly pour in the dry polenta whilst continually whisking with a whisk. Keep on whisking and working those biceps and it will thicken up. It usually takes use takes two minutes for soft polenta, and five for firm.

For firm polenta mix in flavoursome ingredients and pour it into a lightly oiled dish to set. I like to combine chopped sun-dried tomatoes, olives, ground pepper and fresh herbs (basil, thyme, rosemary, parsley, whatever) with my polenta. The polenta can take lots of strong and interesting flavours as it has little flavour itself, so go to town. It sets quickly in the fridge to a nice solid texture. Hey presto! You can turn it out, slice it into wedges and serve with salad or an Italian themed feast.

Another use for firm polenta is to slice it into flat shapes and make polenta pizza. Just add some tomato (fresh or paste) some pizza toppings and a wee bit of cheese and melt.

# Butternut Squash and Feta Tortilla

*This is easy, delicious, and a good source of protein (eggs, nuts, dairy), so it ticks all the right boxes.*

350g cubed butternut squash and sweet potato
Coconut or your favourite oil
1 onion, chopped finely
4 free range organic eggs, beaten
100g feta, cubed
3 tbsp pine nuts

★ Place the cubed squash and sweet potato in lightly oiled baking tray and roast at 200°C until just tender and slightly brown, or about 20 minutes. I use coconut oil to roast them in for an even sweeter flavour.
★ Whilst they're roasting, gently brown the pine nuts in a dry frying pan on a low heat. Place aside.
★ You can use the same frying pan for the tortilla (saves dishes). Use a glug of oil and gently sauté the onion. When the onion is translucent, add the roasted vegetables and stir.
★ Toss in the feta and pour over the beaten eggs. Turn the pan down to a lowish heat, cover and cook until egg has set.
★ Place the frying pan under a medium grill and grill until top is brown. Wrap tin foil around the handle of the pan to prevent it getting burnt under the grill.
★ Serve with a garden salad. If for two people, you can take half for lunch the next day.

# Baked Seasonal Fruit

Having a dinner party and need an easy dessert? Simply run along to a good fruit store and pick up a selection of plums, peaches, figs, pears and apricots – half a fruit per person means that if you buy a variety of five different fruit, everyone will have two and a half fruit each.

Wash, cut in half, de-stone, arrange on a heatproof dish and sprinkle with a bit of vanilla sugar (sugar stored with a vanilla pod in). Pop it into an oven preheated to 220°C for about 5 minutes (pears may take longer) until softened. Serve with a dollop of low fat crème fraiche. Easy.

# Resisting Temptation Hints of the Month

## Pack Your Own

Pack your own lunch every day for a week and see how much money you save. By packing your own lunch, you can more easily control your diet and not fall prey to crisps or chocolate cravings.

Remember to pack something tasty and healthy to nibble on for morning tea. A mid morning snack will keep your metabolism ticking over and keep you on form until lunchtime.

## Ban the Box

Despite the darker evenings, avoid evening television and all the advertisements for chocolate and snack food. Do something constructive, like go out for a walk, investigate evening classes, read a book or pack a tasty lunch for the next day. Once you have weaned yourself off your evening tellie fix, you'll wonder how you wasted so much time in front of the box.

## Portion Control

Most folk feel compelled to finish eating what's on their plate even if they're already full. This is especially true in restaurants. If you are wishing to lose weight, one of the first things you need to realise is that you don't need to eat all the food you're served. It is more sensible to leave a little on your plate than shovel it all down and feel bloated.

Find eateries that serve smaller portions upon request. Alternatively try restaurants that allow you to take a 'doggy bag'. Also, try restaurants that serve traditionally smaller dishes, like Spanish tapas or Turkish meze. Once you've found a good, healthy restaurant, keep their business card so you can recommend it to your friends, family or work colleagues next time you go out for dinner. Dining out need not be a reason to blow your good intentions.

# Fad or Fab

## Pocketfit Playing Cards

It's true, sometime repetitive fitness programmes can get a little boring, so it's fun to mix things up a little. That's probably why there are so many fitness innovations on the market. Pocketfit Cards are exercise cards that double up as playing cards with different exercises and numbers of reps for each card. For a unique workout, shuffle the cards and do the exercise / reps shown. You can either do the whole pack, or try ten minutes to get through as many cards as you can. I've tried them and like them, my guinea pig friend liked the gambling aspect and was exhausted after it. A bit of fun to spice up workouts, but I reckon after a few casino workouts it gets a bit faddish.

## Wii Fit

There's a fad that's been sweeping living rooms everywhere… Wii Fit. It's an ingenious device based on a 'balance board' that a player stands on, that senses the weight distribution through the player's bare feet. In the case of Wii jogging, the remote controller is popped into a pocket which senses leg movement as the player tried to keep up with the 'Mii' jogging around a virtual island. In other words the computer game senses the player's movements that becomes part of the game. Ingenious, yes, but effective? I'm not so sure.

I have a number of issues with the Wii (not only the fact I strained a shoulder in an over-exuberant late-night Wii boxing session at a friend's house). Encouraging consumers to watch a screen to get fit encourages them to stay indoors and look once again to their television for a solution. Health warnings on the Nintendo website include seizures (about 1 in 4,000 chance), repetitive strain injury, eyestrain, electric shock, motion sickness amongst others. I have also met a lady who was hospitalised with a serious back injury from throwing herself across her kitchen in an enthusiastic bout of Wii tennis. It makes cycling through Edinburgh traffic look positively tame.

I reckon for long-term benefit you're better off paying for a block of personal training sessions and learning how to exercise safely and effectively and get outdoors in the fresh air.

# Exercise Of The Month: Swimming

Swimming is a wonderful exercise for streamlining the body and improving your lung capacity and function. Take a break from your lengths and grab a kickboard for a few laps.

Kick furiously at the top of the water, making a splash, and feel the bubbles tingling down your legs. It's a fun and effective exercise for toning the thighs.

A book I highly recommend for anyone starting swimming (or to enhance your swim stroke) is *Total Immersion* by Terry Laughlin. It explains how to swim better, faster and easier in simple language with big writing.

# October Articles

## Effective Exercise

Hang around an aerobics studio or the cardio machines in any gym and you will see some punters thrashing themselves, working up a sweat so intense that you wonder if they will ever recover. It's easy to assume that this is the way we are meant to exercise – raising our heart rates to such an extreme that we turn bright red and feel like we're about to explode. But does it do us any good?

The answer is both yes… and no. As a Western society, we generally assume that harder must be better, after all, we are encouraged to work hard and play hard. Here's good news for you; it's also about working and playing smarter.

Raising your heart rate burns calories, but the type of calories you burn depends on how high your heart rate is. Go too high and you utilise more of your 'in extremis' power supply – that is, burning carbohydrates (stored muscle glycogen) rather than fats. Too low and you're not really burning much at all.

An alternative is to aim for is the elusive 'fat bump', the level at which we burn fat the most effectively. "Where is my fat bump?" I can hear you shouting. To burn fat effectively you need to be active for at least 30 minutes continually, at least three times per week. That's the bare minimum. Ideally you need to be exercising for longer, and more often. But the best bit if you don't need to feel like you're going to puke. Actually slowing down a bit and going for longer will have a greater effect on reducing your waistline. The pace to move at is so you feel puffed. Maintaining this speed for 30 minutes or more will help build your aerobic fitness base.

And this is exactly how we undertake fat burning training. It is at a lower heart rate, but for a longer time. Each individual has a different rate at which they need to train, dependant on age and fitness levels. The most convenient way to fit this into your life is by commuting to work by bike or foot and trying some nice long meanders on the weekend.

It's good to know alternatives exists…

## These Boots Are Made for (Hill) Walking

Scotland has some amazing hills and mountains to explore, and if your walk is longer than two hours (one hour up and one hour down), then you are also getting an excellent 'fat burning' workout that will tone your bum and thighs. Surely a good reason to pull those walking boots on. Here are a few basic tips to get you started:

★ Preparation is key, plan your route and calculate the distance and how long you estimate it will take. Be realistic in what you can achieve for your fitness level and experience and enjoy the walk even more.

★ If it's off the beaten track, invest in an OS (Ordinance Survey) map and compass.

★ Let someone know where you are going and when you expect to be back.

★ Check the weather forecast. Even if it's forecast to be fine, take a waterproof jacket and extra fast wicking layer as it will be colder, wetter and windier on top of a hill. See photo.

★ Invest in some good walking boots and waterproof trousers. Look for these items in sales and you can save a lot of money on kit.

★ Have a preparatory trial run of new equipment and boots on a short walk.

★ Take drinks with you. I like to take a refillable sports bottle of water and some boxes of Ribena (for an instant energy boost).

★ Take a combination of low and high GI snacks so you have slow release energy as well as some 'pick me ups'. Oatcakes, nuts, dark chocolate, home made flapjacks and wholegrain sandwiches are good for slow burning energy, whilst ginger biscuits, peppermints and sugary sweets will give you a burst of energy.

★ Always eat a good breakfast before heading out.

★ Take a survival bag (good for sitting on), mobile phone and whistle. A hat, scarf and gloves will keep you toasty warm.

★ Take extra plastic bags to carry your rubbish, sit on or keep things waterproof.

★ Stop as often as you need, and ensure you stay well hydrated. It's always a good excuse to stop and look at the view.

Check out the Ramblers Association (www.ramblers.org.uk) website for more information.

Here are some ideas specifically on getting fit to tackle the great outdoors.

If you're a gym bunny, get on a stepper to really train your glutes and quads (bum and thighs). Alternatively do a long fast walk on a treadmill with the incline up up up. In addition to cardio (pulse raising) training, strength training is also important. A bums, tums and thighs class is a good place to start if you need ideas for developing leg strength.

Now, a quick word on technique – when walking uphill, walk along ridges rather than valleys as they tend to be drier and easier to walk up.

Everyone has a different walking style. For instance when I'm walking with my (rather tall) husband off piste, I take smaller steps and so look for a different route. Take your time and let the leader know if you're struggling to keep up. Take rests as often as you need to enjoy the scenery and also to refuel and rehydrate.

And finally, after the walk, a nice bath and hearty low fat high protein feast both go down a treat.

## Your Own Home Exercise Space

I like gyms. Honestly, I do, I just rarely bother to get to one (naughty me). I'd rather exercise from home, where it doesn't matter what I look like, I can listen to my music and I don't need to worry about getting there and back. Here are my top ten items to look at if you'd like to start exercising from home:

1.  **Heart Rate Monitor:** Essential for making your cardio exercise measureable. It's an advantage the gyms used to have over home exercise as they used to be mega-pricey. You can now get an entry level Polar model for around £40.

2.  **Exercise Mat:** Essential if you have floorboards or slate underfoot. Carpet is OK to exercise on as long as you don't mind sweating on it and getting covered in fluff. Yoga mats are thin and non slip, and Pilates mats are thicker.

3.  **Trainers:** Your shoes should reflect what you want to do. Many people feel they need to buy fancy shoes to start, but as long as they are comfortable, you're fine. My personal way of finding out if I need a new pair of trainers is by slipping one hand inside an old shoe and placing the other on the sole. If it feels hard and squashed thin as if there is no cushioning, it could be time to buy a new pair, especially if you're running on roads.

4.  **Music:** Create a playlist of your favourite tunes to motivate and inspire you, and most importantly to keep you going when the going gets tough. You can also download exercise podcasts from the internet for something different.

5.  **Resistance Tubes and Bands:** If you travel a lot or don't want to clutter up your home with weights, try using some rubber resistance.

6.  **Cardio Equipment:** All effective exercise programmes involve pulse-raising exercise, which can be measured using your HRM (Heart Rate Monitor). Popular choices include swimming, cycling, running, power walking (although make sure your heart rate is high enough), aerobics or using a bouncer.

7.  **Skipping Rope:** A cheap piece of kit that will get your heart rate up, anywhere, anytime. Generally unsuitable for furnished flats.

8.  **Exercise Ball:** Dependent on space you have available, an exercise ball is very good for core exercises and is also fun. Be sure to buy the 'anti burst' type as cheap balls are horrible and difficult to control (and can also burst). The easy way to tell if it's good quality is that the rubber should be thick and non-reflective.

9.  **Dumbbells:** Hand weights are very useful if a) you know how to use them, and b) you have the correct weight. Dumbbells (individual hand weights) are more versatile than a barbell (a long pole with weights on each end), and easier to store.

10. **Reebok Step:** This is one of my favourite pieces of home exercise kit. You don't need to be an aerobics whizz to benefit from using a step. It's an easy way to get your heart rate up indoors, and it also doubles as a weights bench. Squats and lunges also take on new meaning when done on a step. In an emergency, it can also double as extra seating at a party.

11. **For the Ladies:** A good sports bra is an absolute essential. Not only will it prevent you from taking an eye out, but it will improve your posture, speed and agility.

## Motivation – An Essential Ingredient for Keeping in Shape

A sense of motivation is absolutely essential in a successful fitness programme, in fact is essential for success of any kind. To have motivation you need an end goal in mind. For instance, some people have a goal of having lots of money, so are motivated to work hard. Some people have a sporting goal, and so their sports training has a definite purpose.

**Step 1:** To be motivated you need a purpose and a timeframe. What exactly is your end goal? What do you want to achieve? Is it weight loss (or more correctly fat loss), or do you want to beat your best time? Defining what you want to achieve, and by when, is imperative to your training.

**Step 2:** Recognise that to reach your goal you need prepare and train. After all, it wouldn't be a goal if you were already there. Plan your training and write it in your diary.

**Step 3:** Realise that every single run / fitness session / game practice is getting you closer to your goal, and so is a crucial part of your overall plan. If you lack motivation on the day, visualise your goal. Doing something about it is better than procrastinating.

Many people spend more time procrastinating than it would take them to actually do the exercise. You can always say to yourself that it's better to get it over and done with and feel virtuous for taking positive action. Chances are you'll start enjoying yourself as soon as you start exercising (it's the endorphins).

**Step 4:** Enjoy it! If you are not enjoying your training, perhaps you have set the wrong goal. There are loads of different activities out there, not everyone enjoys running, for instance. Try something different…

**Step 5:** Reward yourself. When you have reached your goal, give yourself a pat on the back. Then set a new goal. It's also OK to have a few weeks off training, then start from the beginning again.

## Running Naked

Got your attention? Here's some information on running barefoot (feet naked). Even if it's not as exciting as running through green fields in the nude, it's a fascinating topic nonetheless.

Feet are amazing. The arch of your foot is designed like the Forth Road Bridge, with a complex arrangement of tendons and ligaments holding the arch up. Anyone who studied science at school will know that the arch shape is one of nature's most effective supports. So if you imagine the amount of weight that goes through your foot, and the fact it's counterbalanced by this wonderful natural arch, you can start to understand the principles of why it's good for your feet to go barefoot. The arch of your foot is built to absorb shock and tension, and if the arch is supported by a lot of cushioned shoe, it may not get to do the job it was designed for.

I learnt lots about feet in *Born to Run* by Christopher McDougall. The book questions why more and more runners nowadays are getting injured, even though the human body was built to run. Yes, we're built to run, according to a popular theory about how humans have evolved to hunt prey by running it down. Humans, unlike most mammals, are able to radiate body heat through our non-furry skin. Our unique ability to sweat means that we can keep pursuing prey without having to stop to cool down (as in the case of many mammals that only expire heat through panting). So our skeletal framework, tendons, ligaments and other bits and pieces are designed so we can pursue our hunt prey not by speed, but by persistence. We are designed to be slow plodders.

It is interesting that historically we never wore big spongy running shoes. Ironically running shoes with lots of cushioning (to protect the legs from the impact of running on tarmac) can actually exacerbate leg injuries. Running on tarmac is not a natural thing to do. Full stop. 'Pounding the pavement' in squishy shoes really is a bit bizarre when you think about it. The squishier the shoe, the more likely you are to run heavily. If you want to know your natural running style, kick off your shoes and run about your house. You will find your foot lands, or strikes, differently. It's not particularly feasible or desirable to run around urban areas with no shoes on, so what to do?

If you live in a city and like running outside, then generally you will do it on tarmac. If you run on tarmac, then it's generally advisable to wear protection as tarmac is a hard surface. That doesn't mean knee pads in case you fall over, although this might be handy. No, protection means wearing squishy shoes that will help absorb the impact that reverberates up the shin. Heard of shin splints? Shin splints can be caused from too much impact going through the lower leg. You are less likely to get sore legs if you run on a natural surface; dirt absorbs the impact of a foot strike more than rock hard tarmac.

In reaction to this, the squishy running shoe has recently been pared down to a minimal model. The premise of this new running shoe, as championed by British brand Innov8, is that less cushioning means you will run more in your own natural style. However, and this is a big however, minimal running shoes are designed mainly to be worn for off road running.

Another shoe in the new minimal genre is the strange shoes with toes on, otherwise known as Vibram Five Fingers. I call them 'yeti shoes' as they are most unbecoming on the feet. If you'd like to join the minimal movement, wear them around the house before trialling uncushioned shoes on a short run, gradually increasing the distance

It's a case of those eternal swings and roundabouts. I do know two facts: running on tarmac requires cushioning and secondly, extra cushioning may change your running style. So, if you can find a field or a beach to run along barefoot – go for it. Otherwise, pull your squishy shoes on and go for a comfy run… and spend some time at home (feet) naked.

# NOVEMBER

Darker nights can be off-putting for exercising outdoors, but remember that there are plenty of folk exercising in the dark. Getting outdoors over the darker months can help boost your mood and combat winter glumness. If running in the dark isn't your thing, be sure to get out for a brisk walk at lunch and capture some Vitamin D.

## WHAT'S IN SEASON

**Apples, blackberries, pears, plums, elderberries (in the wild), figs, beetroot, butternut squash, courgettes, Jerusalem artichokes, kale, kohlrabi, leeks, marrow, mushrooms, potatoes, pumpkin, rocket, wild mushrooms, radishes, fennel, onions, squash, swede, watercress.**

## OATCAKE TOPPING OF THE MONTH

Sometimes it's nice to have a bit of cheese on oatcakes, so for a seasonal change try a sliver of blue cheese with a slice of pear. Rather yummy, and it's easier to have less cheese when you have a slice of fruit with it. Apple also works well and cuts through the creaminess of the cheese.

# Easy Autumn Recipes

## Butternut Squash Soup

*Serves four*

2 butternut squash
Olive or coconut oil
1 onion, chopped
1 clove garlic, crushed
1 litre vegetable stock
Natural yoghurt and a sprinkle of nutmeg for serving

★ Preheat oven to 200°C.
★ Chop the top and bottom off the squash, then cut into halves and scrape out the seeds with a spoon.
★ Cut into large chunks, chop off the skin and place on a lightly oiled oven tray.
★ Roast the squash in the oven for 20 minutes or until tender.
★ Sauté the onion and garlic in a little olive or coconut oil, and then add the squash and enough stock to cover.
★ Cook on a low heat for a few minutes, allowing the flavours to infuse.
★ Take off the heat. Blend until smooth, then reheat.
★ Serve with a dollop of yoghurt and a sprinkle of nutmeg.

## Everyone's Crazy for Quinoa

Britain's gone quinoa (pronounced keen-wah) crazy. It's the seed of the quinoa plant that is used, and it's the texture of these seeds as they pop in your mouth that make quinoa so tasty. It's a bit like couscous but nuttier. It's been grown in South America for over 6,000 years and thanks to the global nature of British culinary trends, has made it's way over here… Most quinoa is imported from Bolivia. High on air miles.

To quote the ever reliable Wikipedia:

"Quinoa was of great nutritional importance in pre-Columbian Andean civilizations, being secondary only to the potato, and was followed in importance by maize. In contemporary times, this crop has become highly appreciated for its nutritional value, as its protein content is very high (12%–18%), making it a healthful choice for vegetarians and vegans. Unlike wheat or rice (which are low in lysine), quinoa contains a balanced set of essential amino acids for humans, making it an unusually complete protein source. It is a good source of dietary fiber and phosphorus and is high in magnesium and iron. Quinoa is gluten-free and considered easy to digest. Because of all these characteristics, quinoa is being considered a possible crop in NASA's Controlled Ecological Life Support System for long-duration manned space flights." Wow.

It's certainly a good high protein cereal option for active vegetarians who would like a change from rice and pasta. It doesn't have a huge amount of flavour and goes with pretty much anything, so you can go to town on flavourings.

Cook it in a saucepan with one part quinoa to two parts boiling water. If you cook 1 cup of dried quinoa to 2 cups of water, it makes 2 ½ cups of cooked quinoa. Like couscous, it will absorb the water, so bring to the boil and simmer on a low heat for 10 to 15 minutes or until all the water is absorbed. Use the cooked quinoa to make the following recipes.

## Quinoa Burgers

*Makes six burgers*

1½ cups cooked quinoa, cooled
2 organic free-range eggs
¼ cup plain flour
2 shallots, chopped (or any onion)
Breadcrumbs
Handful chopped fresh herbs (ideally coriander)
Any other seasoning you like (we like cumin)
Some grated cheese, if you're feeling devilish
Coconut or olive oil for cooking

★ Combine all of the above (except the oil) in a mixing bowl. Add as many breadcrumbs as you need to make the mixture sticky but not dry.
★ Cook on a medium heat in non stick frying pan with a smidge of oil. Turn carefully after two minutes.
★ Serve with a salad and lots of chilli sauce.

# Quinoa Green Curry

*Serves two*

*So simple, and the cashews and quinoa are both good sources of vegetable protein.*

2 cups of diced vegetables (an assortment of carrots, sweet potato, courgette, potato, onion, beans)
Handful raw cashew nuts
3 tbsp green curry paste
Additional spices are optional, i.e. chilli, garlic, ginger, holy basil, coriander
1 tbsp coconut oil
1 tin coconut milk
1 cup cooked quinoa
Wedges of lime, finely chopped spring onions and fresh coriander leaves

★ Fry off the curry paste in a little oil and add onions, then add the rest of the vegetables and sauté until aromatic.
★ Add the coconut milk.
★ Cook on a medium heat until nearly done.

★ 5 minutes before serving, mix the curry, quinoa and cashews together in a pot on a low heat.

★ Garnish with spring onions, coriander leaves and a wedge of lime for squeezing.

## Lazy Quinoa Porridge

*This is a good method to use up leftover quinoa, and you can add whatever ingredients you like to taste.*

★ Place leftover cooked and cooled quinoa into a plastic container.

★ Add a splash of milk to cover, a sprinkle of mixed spice, some honey, dried cranberries and some toasted and ground almonds (or whatever you prefer).

★ Refrigerate overnight.

★ In the morning simply microwave the whole container, or heat in a pan.

★ A surprisingly palatable alternative to porridge…

## Andy's Veggie Spaghetti Bolognaise

Veggie mince (otherwise known by the brand name of Quorn) is a great occasional high protein, low fat option. It's especially delicious in this quick and easy spag bol recipe perfected by my husband Andy. It's a great meal to refuel on after a busy day as the protein will help aid muscle recovery. Serve with wholemeal spaghetti, which has more protein and three times the fibre of ordinary spaghetti.

*Serves four*

1 onion, finely chopped
1 – 4 cloves of garlic, crushed
2 tbsp olive oil
200g veggie mince (or Quorn)
1 red pepper, cut into medium squares
1 medium fresh chilli, sliced finely
Handful of mushrooms, sliced coarsely
Oregano, thyme and / or mixed herbs
Tin of chopped tomatoes
100ml vegetable stock
1 packet wholemeal spaghetti

* In a large covered saucepan heat the olive oil to a medium heat and sweat the onion and garlic.
* When softened, stir in the veggie mince (you can cook from frozen), chopped vegetables and herbs, and fry for awhile.
* Add the tin of chopped tomatoes and the stock and let it reduce on a lowish heat for about 20 minutes.
* Start cooking the spaghetti and remember that wholemeal takes longer than 'ordinary' spag.
* This recipe keeps in the fridge well, and makes a tasty reheated lunch.

## Dolmades (Vine Leaf Rolls)

125g short grain rice, cooked, rinsed, drained and cooled
1 lemon, juiced
Small handful of mint and parsley, finely chopped
Sea salt and freshly ground pepper
Vine leaves (available from a global grocer)
Olive oil and lemon juice to taste

* Combine all of the above ingredients, except vine leaves.
* Lay a vine leaf shiny side down on a chopping board and remove the largest veins, as they are chewy.
* Squeeze a small amount of the rice mixture in your hand and place in the middle of the vine leaf.
* Roll, wrapping the sides of the vine leaf in, so the rice is contained in the leaf (similar to how they wrap hot chips at a chippie).
* Arrange dolmades on a plate that is covered with vine leaves and drizzle lightly with olive oil and lemon juice. Chill before eating.

## Easy Vegetable Pie

*Makes four slices*

2 potatoes, finely diced
2 carrots, finely diced
2 shallots or 1 onion
½ cup frozen peas
1 tbsp olive oil
Black pepper

100ml vegetable stock

Fresh herbs (perhaps thyme, rosemary and a couple bay leaves)

Tiny bit crushed / fresh chilli (optional)

1 packet puff pastry, or shortcrust if you prefer.

1 tbsp sesame seeds

★ Preheat oven to 200ºC.

★ In a pan, sauté the shallots / onions on a medium heat in the oil, add the carrots and potatoes and stir through.

★ After a couple of minutes, add a dash of vegetable stock (enough to keep it moist, but not so it's swimming in it), herbs, chilli and pepper.

★ Cover and simmer until veggies are tender.

★ Roll the puff pastry on a floured board into a large rectangle. Position the pastry in a pie dish and heap the filling in the middle, wrap the pastry around it so the seam is at the top.

★ Brush with a little milk and sprinkle on sesame seeds.

★ Cook in the over for 30 minutes or until pastry is browned.

Serve with lots of steamed vegetables. Aim for a middle piece (with less pastry and more filling) for yourself. The leftovers also make a perfect take-to-work lunch.

## Homemade Cold Repellent

It's also the time of year when colds and coughs rear their ugly head. Plenty of rest and making sure you make time to relax are important in keeping the gremlins at bay, but it's also a good excuse to drink hot lemon and honey drink. Simply squeeze half a lemon into a mug and add a spoon of honey. Half fill with boiling water, stir and enjoy. You can add a slice of fresh ginger for an extra warming effect.

My personal method of curing colds is to very finely chop a clove of fresh garlic, put it on a spoon and swallow it with a big glass of water. The trick is not to chew it or let it touch your teeth, this way it shouldn't really affect your breath. Scary, but effective.

# Resisting Temptation Hints of the Month

## Not So Supermarkets

It's an old one, but a good one: write a shopping list when you go shopping. And stick to it. See if you can pick up your groceries from smaller local shops, which are often as cheap and without queues.

## Fruit First

It is quite common to snack at work to relieve stress or boredom. At these times we tend to reach for sugary snacks that give us a temporary sugar peak, but then an energy dip. Do yourself a favour, and next time you'd like a mid-afternoon biscuit or sweet, have an apple first.

Try saying to yourself "I'll have that biscuit after I've eaten an apple". Not only does this help you get your five a day, but you'll probably have forgotten about the biscuit by the time you've eaten the apple.

## A Simple Way to Cut Calories

Do you like things sweet? How much sugar do you add?

Try halving that and half your calories.

You may not even taste the difference.

# Fad or Fab

## Ice Baths

There's a recent trend for folk post-exercise to immerse themselves in an ice cold bath. The premise of this is similar to the classic R.I.C.E. (rest, ice, compression, elevation) treatment for injuries and sprains and strains. Cooling the injured area causes the blood vessels to constrict and blood to leave the affected area, thereby reducing inflammation and promoting healing. This is a similar concept as compression tights. Now, I don't know about you, but the idea of sitting in a pool of ice cold water after exercise doesn't really appeal to me.

So, where does the blood go? The heart, one would imagine. Perhaps not a good idea for some. In a recent fitness magazine article, it was also recommended to wear a hat to avoid hypothermia. It strikes me as a particularly unsafe practice. If you have an injury or cramp, apply a localised cold compress. You sure won't find me sitting in ice, unless it's 30 degrees plus outside. No siree, a nice warm bath with Epsom salts, a cup of herbal tea and compression leggings for me… I hope this is a fad.

## Pedometer

There are a wide variety of inexpensive pedometers on the market that work on the principle of measuring the number of steps the wearer takes. To do this, it is clipped to the waistband and it measures how many times it is jiggled by the wearer's leg. This theoretically measures the number of steps the wearer makes. The downfall of this design is that when you go to the loo, it measures it as steps, if you jump and up down, it's also measured as steps. So it is really an approximate reading. Some models also automatically calculate the theoretical distance covered. This is assuming that the wearer takes the same length strides each time.

Whilst a pedometer may be an inexpensive way to calculate if the wearer has been moving around enough in a day, it's not a terribly accurate way of doing it. With the advent of GPS on mobile phones, and route mapping technology, pedometers will be relegated to the back of the cupboard.

## Exercise Of The Month: Even Your Load

Do you always carry your shopping or handbag on one side only? Most of us favour a dominant side, and use this side to do most heavy lifting and carrying. This can lead to uneven distribution of strength and crookedness of posture.

To help alleviate this, try carrying bags with your non-dominant side. You may find yourself unconsciously shifting the load back to your stronger side, but it's good to try and persist with it. It can feel a little weird to start, so perhaps say to yourself "I'll carry the shopping with my weaker side up to this junction". You can build up, so you're eventually using your non-dominant side to carry your shopping half way home. Before long, this side will strengthen and become almost as strong as your dominant side.

# November Articles

## And Breathe...

How many times a minute do you breathe? I bet you don't know. It's something we do day in day out without thinking. We have to, but why exactly?

Breathing is the body's way of ridding itself of waste, a.k.a. carbon dioxide and to take in fuel, oxygen. Breathing is something we do unconsciously, it's hard wired into our system by signals from the nervous system to the diaphragm, the big sheet of muscle that horizontally divides the rib cage. As the diaphragm contracts, the space in the chest cavity expands and so air goes rushing in. Air is made up of about 20% oxygen, which is absorbed into the blood stream through the tiny finger-like alveoli in the lungs. Oxygen jumps onto a haemoglobin 'taxi' in the blood and is pumped by the heart to the far reaches of the body, where it is then used as a fuel to convert into energy. If you think of how oxygen

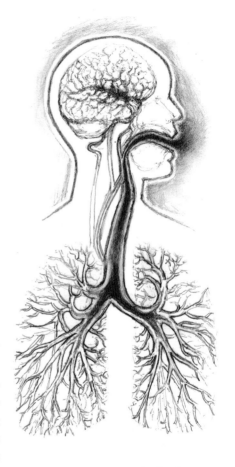

helps a fire burn, you get the general idea. So without oxygen, the body cannot function. Actually most of the body may be OK for awhile without oxygen, but the brain would die. So a good argument for thinking about your breathing.

The rate of breathing is dictated by the requirement of the body. As you exercise, your whole body moves and therefore requires more fuel (and therefore oxygen), so your breathing rate increases accordingly. Clever hey? Your body also produces more carbon dioxide as a by-product of producing energy, which needs to be carted away and back to the lungs to be exhaled. When you sleep, your breathing slows down. It all makes a lot of sense.

So I ask you, why is not more emphasis placed on learning how to breathe effectively to help your body function better? Why do we not learn this at school? A heart rate monitor is a useful tool for learning more about your breathing. It's quite fascinating to watch how heart rate increases as exercise intensity increases. The fitter you are, the more effectively you use the air you breathe in. Firstly, your lung capacity increases so you can breathe in more air in one breath, and secondly, the stronger your heart (cardiac muscle) is, the more effectively you pump blood around the body.

Therefore the fitter you are, the lower your resting heart rate. Which means your heart doesn't need to pump as many times to do the same amount of work. There are many things that can put your heart rate up, including going up a hill (more effort), or into the wind (very Edinburgh), drinking caffeine (a stimulant), a cold or fever (as your body is already working hard to fight the infection), a hangover (your body ridding itself of toxins) or smoking (as the lungs don't work so well in transferring oxygen). Also folk with high blood pressure tend to have a higher heart rate as their heart may work less effectively, especially if blood vessels are hardened or clogged with fatty deposits.

So how can you breathe more effectively? You may think it's completely daft when I recommend that you practise breathing. If you're feeling a little stressed, or out of breath walking up hills, practise taking in some deep breaths. Do this by thinking about expanding your rib cage, rather than gasping. What you will be effectively doing is delivering more oxygen as fuel to your body, which will in turn make your body work better, faster, stronger – just like the Daft Punk song.

Breathing correctly is not only important in energetic exercise, but also when stretching. Muscle fibres actually need oxygen to lengthen, which is why breathing is such an important aspect of yoga. If you think about it hard enough, you will also figure out that as your brain requires oxygen to function, getting more oxygen in will logically 'clear your head' and help with difficult problems. So next time you're faced with an annoying work problem, or writer's block, leap up from your desk and escape for a fast walk or a bit of a jog outdoors, get the oxygen in, and make yourself even smarter.

## Winter Fitness Ideas

At this time of year it's especially important to get creative regarding your fitness programme. Here are some winter ideas to get you all warmed up:

★ Invest in some high viz running clothes and train towards a summer race. Try running at different times during the day, or do one long run outdoors on the weekend and shorter weekday runs on a treadmill if you don't like running in the dark.

★ If you continue cycling in the dark, remember to be highly visible and that a motorist has not seen you until they have made eye contact with you. Assume that motorists aren't looking out for you and you should be safe.

★ If you prefer to cycle in the comfort of your living room, invest in a Turbo Trainer that converts a bike to exercise bike.

★ Continuing the indoors theme, take up a yoga / dance / Pilates class. Aerobics classes are also a fun way to get fit indoors, especially if you rope in a friend. Kickboxing is also a brilliant all round fitness kick.

★ Swimming: it doesn't matter if it's raining outdoors, you're going to get wet anyway. Find somewhere with a sauna to truly relax afterwards. This is a favourite trick of many Antipodeans during a Scottish winter. Get hot and sweaty in a sauna, and try not to look at Australian weather forecasts.

★ Utilise your DVD club membership and hire some exercise videos to while away a dark evening.

## Are You Seasonally Affected? Or Are You Just Lazy?

SAD (Seasonal Affective Disorder) is meant to only affect a small percentage of our population. However every winter I encounter many folk who find their energy levels dipping with the light levels. Whilst there may be a certain number of people suffering from the 'disorder' of SAD, we all feel it more or less depending on our gender, country of origin, and flexibility of our working lives.

Over winter I notice a definite dropping of enthusiasm as the light levels are reduced to about six hours of daylight (and none, except for lunchtime, during the week for office workers). Through winter many people want to be indoors, not necessarily for the warmth, but in my opinion, more for cheery light.

The amount of sunlight we get directly correlates to mood and energy levels.

The turnover of the 'feel good' neurotransmitters melatonin and serotonin in the brain is directly related to sunlight and therefore is lowest in winter. This varies from individual to individual, but explains why we can feel glum during December.

Also, our climate shapes our culture. Whilst Australia has a largely outdoor leisure culture, the UK has one of being indoors more. Generally the British are great conversationalists partially because of the culture of sitting around indoors together chatting. In Australia, traditionally people were on the beach and outdoors doing stuff. However, it should be noted that nowadays Australia has a larger obesity problem then the UK. I blame technological advances in air conditioning…

One thing I love about Edinburgh is the impossibly long days of summer. Having grown up in Australia, these long evenings seem almost magical. I carry those memories around in my head through winter and look forward to the next summer.

A successful fitness programme in Britain needs to consider the light levels. Even professional athletes take regular breaks from their training. Do you alter your own fitness programme to fit in with the seasons? If you find going to the gym in the morning in the dark difficult, consider going after work, or even on the weekend. See if you can use your lunchtimes to get outside and get active.

Professional athletes have competitions or sporting seasons to work towards, so there is no reason why 'leisure trainers' should not have the same focus. At this time of year it's handy to have a goal to work towards. A common goal is looking good for festive celebrations and Hogmanay. Perhaps you can treat yourself to a new outfit and banish the winter blues by looking and feeling great.

Once you have worked towards this goal, then take a week or two planned rest from your programme (perhaps time off over Christmas when the weather is at it's darkest). By structuring your fitness routine like this, you are always working towards a goal or giving yourself a well-earned, planned break.

Then, at the beginning of the new year you can set a new goal and work towards that. Summer holidays anyone?

# Untangling Yoga

Yoga is a wonderful way to unwind and relax, to forget about your worries and regain a sense of inner peace. Forget about traffic jams, screaming kids, the busy office, looming deadlines and any other trifling matters that might be whirling around your head. It's a chance to be at one with your body and your breath.

Yoga is based upon a series of physical postures (called poses), which vary in difficulty and speed of execution, depending on the style. Some styles are fast and flowing, others are slow and relaxing.

Are you confused and unsure where to start? Worry not, for following is your very own guide to decoding yoga styles.

**Hatha Yoga:** Hatha yoga is slow and relaxing with the teacher talking you through poses that focus on breath and getting a really good stretch. It's a good introduction to yoga and is great for stress relief or if you have stiff muscles. My personal favourite for chilling out…

**Iyengar Yoga:** Based on the teachings of the yogi B.K.S. Iyengar, it focuses on correct body alignment. Iyengar emphasises holding poses for a length of time, rather than the flow of moving from one pose to another (used in Ashtanga yoga).

Iyengar encourages the use of props, such as yoga blankets, blocks and straps to assist bringing the body into alignment. Fabulous for your posture, Iyengar promotes evenness and balance.

**Ashtanga & Power Yoga:** Ashtanga (which means eight limbs in Sanskrit) is a fast-paced, intense style of yoga. A set series of poses is performed, always in the same order. Ashtanga practice is very physically demanding, because of the constant flow from one pose to the next.

Ashtanga is also the inspiration for power yoga. If a class is described as power yoga, it will be based on the flowing style of Ashtanga, but not necessarily keeping strictly to Ashtanga poses.

Both Ashtanga and Power yoga are higher in energy and therefore are likely to burn more calories. The flip side is that they are the yoga practises most likely to cause injury. I have seen clients with strained shoulders from moving too suddenly into the downward dog position, so please be careful when you're starting Ashtanga yoga – go to a beginners class, or even a Hatha yoga class first, to understand the principles of breathing and to improve your flexibility.

**Bikram Yoga:** A method of yoga in a heated rooms (around 40°C), lasting 90 minutes and comprising of a sequence of poses in a specific order. The heat encourages sweating and also allows muscles to relax.

## What is Metabolism?

*"The physical and chemical processes by which substances are produced or transformed (broken down) into energy or products for the uses of the body."*

In other words, your metabolism is the process where nutrients (food) are broken down into useable energy (for movement).

Your metabolic rate is how fast this reaction happens (i.e. how quickly food is broken down into usable energy). A high metabolic rate means that food is 'burnt' more quickly. Which is why we need to aim to increase our metabolic rate. By having a faster metabolic rate, or metabolism, we are able to burn calories more effectively, even at rest. Interestingly, it should also be noted that metabolism decreases with age... One of the myriad of reasons why we change shape with age.

So, how can you increase your metabolism? It's easy.

★ Always eat a decent sized breakfast to kick start your metabolism.

★ Eat five or six small meals throughout the day. You will need to plan ahead a bit more, but it will pay dividends. Also, you will not get hungry and are therefore less likely to snack on junk (crisps, sweets etc). Taper off your food intake over the course of the day, with bigger meals in the morning and smaller in the evening.

★ Undertake cardiovascular exercise (i.e. running, fast walking, cycling, dancing, aerobics) at least three times per week, at an effort where you feel puffed.

★ By building muscle mass. This does not mean you have to bulk up, but instead, convert fat to muscle. Muscle is a metabolically active tissue. It requires a certain number of calories each day to maintain itself. Therefore, the more muscle you have, the more calories you burn even when you're just sitting around. As your muscle mass drops, so does your daily calorie requirement. Exercises which will increase muscle mass are the strength exercises (i.e. press ups, squats, lunges).

★ Drink plenty of water.

# DECEMBER

It's nearing the shortest day and 'silly season'. It's the time of year when many of us feel like hibernating and waiting out the darker months. Sadly we are not little bears so it's crucial to stay active and get outdoors.

## WHAT'S IN SEASON

Apples, beetroot, Brussels sprouts, carrots, celeriac, chestnuts, chicory, Jerusalem artichoke, kale, kohlrabi, leeks, parsnips, pears, potatoes, pumpkin, quince, turnips, red cabbage, sprouts, swede.

## OATCAKE TOPPING OF THE MONTH

Quince paste: You may not have heard of it, but it's a lovely floral tasting jelly otherwise known as membrillo. A relative of the apple, quinces are a native of Persia and are the fruit of love, marriage and fertility… and the paste is also pretty good on oatcakes. Try a sliver with a thin slice of strong tasting cheese and you'll see what I mean. You can pick up quince paste from a fancy delicatessen.

# Easy Winter Recipes

## Roast Chestnuts

Chestnuts are the lowest in calories and fats of all nuts [190 calories, 2.74 g fat per 100 g] and cholesterol free. Chestnuts are high in carbohydrates, balanced in proteins and are an excellent source of trace minerals; they compare with brown rice in nutritional value. In other words, they're a wonderfully healthy winter snack.

Choose shiny bright chestnuts, a sign of freshness. Using a very sharp knife, score a cross on the rounded side of each chestnut. Preheat oven to 200°C and place in an oven tray in the middle shelf. Roast for 20 minutes, then remove and place directly into a bowl lined with a clean tea-towel. Wrap the towel around the chestnuts and leave for 5 – 10 minutes (this helps steam the shells so they loosen). Gently crush down on the towel before unwrapping. Shell and enjoy.

## Roast Vegetable Soup

*Serves four (or two with leftovers to freeze)*

½ celeriac
2 carrots
1 large potato
1 sweet potato
1 tbsp olive oil
1 onion
1 – 4 cloves garlic
Vegetable stock
Coriander or other fresh green herbs

★ Chop the vegetables roughly (you can choose other root vegetables, but try to include celeriac as it adds a lovely fresh flavour to the soup) toss with the olive oil in the biggest roasting pan you have.

★ Place on the middle shelf of your oven on 180°C for 30 minutes.

★ Chop the onion and peel the garlic and mix into the roasting vegetables, leaving the garlic whole.

★ Return to the oven for another 30 minutes or until done but not too crispy.

★ Have a wee nibble on the veg if you wish, then toss the rest into a big saucepan.

- ★ Cover with hot vegetable stock and simmer on a low heat to infuse the flavours.
- ★ Cool and blend. I add fresh coriander before blending, then more after it is zizzed.
- ★ Garnish with fresh herbs and natural yoghurt. This recipe is comforting on a wintry weekend afternoon.

## Squash and Sage Risotto

This a real treat on a chilly night, and the fresh rocket contrasts with the rich creaminess of the risotto. You can always enjoy half for dinner and save some for your lunch as it reheats in a microwave well.

*Serves four, or two dinners and two lunches*

1 large butternut squash
2 tbsp fresh sage, finely chopped (dried is OK, but use less)
2 tbsp olive oil
25g butter
1 onion, finely chopped
2 cloves garlic, finely chopped
300g risotto rice
1 litre vegetable stock
150ml dry white wine or a splash of dry vermouth
2 tbsp pine nuts, dry roasted in a pan (optional)
50g parmesan cheese, grated
A handful of rocket

- ★ Preheat oven to 200°C.
- ★ Peel and dice butternut squash into 1cm cubes.
- ★ Roast in a roasting dish with olive oil and most of the sage on a medium heat for 15 – 20 minutes until tender.
- ★ On a medium heat, melt the butter and 1 tbsp olive oil together in a large heavy bottomed pan, and sauté onion and garlic.
- ★ Add the risotto rice and stir until rice is coated and smells fragrant.
- ★ Lower the heat and add the white wine or vermouth to the rice and stir until absorbed.
- ★ Add a ladle full of vegetable stock at a time, stirring until absorbed.

* When you have used up about a half of the stock, throw in the contents of the roasting pan. You can add a bit of extra sage at this point if you'd like a stronger flavour.
* Continue stirring in the stock bit by bit until it is all absorbed and cubes of squash are slightly squished. You can also add the roast pine nuts at this point.
* Serve with a sprinkle of fresh parmesan cheese and rocket sprinkled on top for a fresh texture.

## Mushroom, Cashew and Tofu Festive Roast

If any of your family or friends are veggie, they'll love you (even more) for going to the effort of making them something special for Christmas. It's not much effort for this yummy loaf, and you can prepare it in advance and cook it on the day.

2 tbsp olive oil
1 onion, finely chopped
2 cloves garlic, crushed
125g wholemeal breadcrumbs, fresh
200 – 250g cashews
300g plain tofu (firm, not silken)
1 tsp rosemary, fresh is best
1 tsp thyme, fresh is best
1 vegetable stock cube
125ml hot water
250g mushrooms, chopped (field mushrooms for maximum taste)
Ground black pepper and sea salt
Greased 2 lb loaf tin

* Preheat oven to 180°C
* In a big pot, heat 1 tbsp olive oil and sauté onion and garlic until soft, not brown. Take off the heat.
* If you're making your own breadcrumbs, you can do this now, then grind the cashews and mix them together.
* Add the cashew / breadcrumb mix to the pot of onion and garlic and toss in the herbs.
* Blend the stock cube, hot water and tofu in a blender until creamy.
* Add the tofu mix to the pan and add salt and pepper to taste.

* In a separate pan, heat remaining oil and sauté the mushrooms.
* In the greased loaf tin, arrange some of the mushrooms, then press in half the tofu / cashew mix.
* Arrange another layer of mushrooms, then the rest of the tofu / cashew mix, then a final layer of mushrooms.
* Seal the top with a piece of tin foil and bake for one hour.
* When cooked, remove from oven and stand for 10 minutes, before easing round edges with a knife and turning out
* Very tasty with roast vegetables and onion gravy.

## Baked Apples

Baked apples are a warming way to end an evening meal. There's something festive about them and they're a great way to use tart old apples. So easy, and the quantities are up to you. It's worth investing a couple of quid in an apple corer just for this recipe.

* In a heatproof container, mix 2 tbsp sultanas with ½ tsp mixed spice, 1 tsp dark brown sugar and ½ tsp butter per apple. Cover with boiling water.

* Let the stuffing mixture sit for awhile. You can go straight to the next step, but if you're preparing this filling in advance, let the sultanas rehydrate prior to cooking.
* Core each apple and make a horizontal cut along the middle so the peel doesn't burst when cooking.
* Fill each empty core with sultana mix. Top with a clove. Pour any sultana mix liquid onto the apples.
* Place in a covered casserole dish and cook at 180°C for 30 minutes.
* Serve with low fat crème fraiche.

# Resisting Temptation Hints of the Month

## Tangerinetastic

Many people find themselves craving something sweet at this time of year. Do yourself a favour and take a tangerine in a wee sandwich bag out with you. The tangerine is a good sweet replacement, packed with vitamin C to help stave off colds, and the plastic bag means it won't get squished in your bag, and you'll have somewhere to dispose of the peel.

## Go Veggie

At a restaurant? Want to eat healthy? Try the vegetarian option. Usually healthier, the vegetarian option is often overlooked by meat eaters but is worthy of your consideration.

## Masticate Well

How fast do you eat? Are you a scoffer or a nibbler? Eating slowly and taking smaller bites can help you lose weight. This happens for a number of reasons.

Firstly, you give your body a better chance to realise when you're satisfied, as it take 30 minutes or so for your brain to register that you've eaten enough. Secondly, you will enjoy your food more as it's not hoovered up in an instant, but relished over time. Lastly if you eat more slowly, you will masticate (chew) more and therefore assist your digestion. Your digestive system actually starts from the moment you put food in your mouth and your saliva gets to work. So avoid an uncomfortable bloated feeling by eating smaller and more considered bites. Especially important over the festive season where there tends to be a lot of sitting around and indulging. Enjoy!

# Fad or Fab

## Balls! (Swiss balls that is)

Swiss balls (or exercise balls) are those big inflatable balls that look like they belong on the beach. Originally used by physiotherapists, they have become increasing popular in gyms and also in the home. They are fun, but are they any good?

Like many things in life Swiss balls are good for some things and not for others. The primary purpose of the ball is to help strengthen your core, the deep muscles in your torso that keep you upright. Like the Power Plate and MBT shoes, the ball works on the theory of putting the user off balance. That is, you really need to use your muscles to balance on the ball.

This is great for deep abdominal strength, however it doesn't necessarily translate to being fab for isolating other muscle groups. In simple terms, if you are doing an arm exercise, chances are you're concentrating so hard on keeping your balance on the ball that you cannot concentrate on the actual exercise. So it's not ideal for targeting specific muscles in the body.

In summary, the ball is great if used some of the time to strengthen abs and inject a bit of fun into a workout.

## Space Hoppers

You can probably guess that Space Hoppers get the big thumbs up for the festive season. These are a great gift for kids, young or old, and you can now buy various sizes of Space Hoppers from many retailers. They've been around since I was a youngster, and I loved nothing more than bouncing along on a 'hopper. Space Hopper races usually end up in hysterics, as the harder you bounce, the higher you go. "So what's this good for?" you may ask. Not only is it great fun, but it's a killer quads workout (like doing dozens of squats) and also uses core muscles to keep your balance in a similar way to the Swiss ball. So if you can get children doing exercises voluntarily, you're helping their future muscle development. The fact is, the fitter the child, the more likely they are to be fit and healthy as an adult. And for adults, we all need a good laugh every now and then. A most definite **FAB**.

## Fast Wicking Clothing

You know the situation, you've worked up a sweat but as soon as you cool down from a run or a cycle in your soggy gear, you freeze. Advances in technology mean that this no longer needs to be the case. Try a 'fast wicking' synthetic blend of fabric, which draws moisture away from the body, so you dry off quicker. Handy in hot weather, but even more valuable in the depths of winter where you don't want your muscles to freeze up after a workout. Fast wicking clothing is available from outdoor shops. A fast wicking shirt under a warm fleece with a waterproof shell jacket on top is all you need for running about in the winter. Also be sure to buy tops with zips so you are better able to control your body temperature. It's much more comfortable than soggy cotton layers. Fast wicking clothes get the two thumbs up. Now all they need to do is make some fashionable robust fleeces.

## Exercise of the Month: Pump It

If you have a Swiss ball, pump it up and have a play. It's a fun form of indoor exercise, and can be a real challenge for your core stomach muscles if used properly. Many Swiss balls come with an exercise chart, but do check with someone who knows that you are doing the exercises correctly.

# December Articles

## Damage Control Over Christmas

- ★ Keep on exercising – it will burn off the rich food of the season, keep your festive spirits up and you'll have less to regret come New Year.
- ★ Have fresh fruit juice in the fridge and fresh fruit in a fruit bowl at all times.
- ★ Often the vegetarian option for work dinners are the healthiest. Consider them, and give them a try.
- ★ Always eat breakfast on Christmas day as this will fill you up and you will be less likely to snack on Christmas fayre.
- ★ Serve Christmas dinner with heaps of vegetables for a balanced meal that helps toward your five servings of fruit or veg a day.
- ★ Steam or roast vegetables to preserve more vitamins. Serve without salt, using other flavourings like lemon, pepper or fresh herbs instead
- ★ Cut potatoes for roasting into larger chunks – they'll absorb less fat. Roast in a small amount of vegetable-based oil for a healthier choice. Or even try coconut oil for an exotic alternative.
- ★ Try making your own gravy instead of using cubes or granules that tend to be higher in salt.
- ★ Serve the traditional Christmas pudding with try some natural yoghurt, crème fraiche or even some fresh fruit.

- ★ Avoid sugary fizzy drinks and opt for water or fruit juice with a slice of lemon or lime.
- ★ Sit away from the buffet table, making sure you can only reach healthy snacks. Move unhealthy snacks to out of reach or replace with healthier nibbles (almonds, seeds, pretzels).
- ★ Go for a stroll to burn off a heavy lunch. The extra oxygen will also clear your head.
- ★ Drink a glass of water for every glass of wine you imbibe
- ★ Consider taking milk thistle, a herbal relative of the artichoke, which has been proved to have liver-assisting properties.
- ★ If you do over indulge, don't punish yourself, just launch yourself straight back into your healthy version of living and consider it a learning experience. What are your new year's goals?

## Stuck for Christmas Presents?

Christmas can be a wonderful time of giving and sharing. What kind of gifts do you give? We all know that it's good to be fit and healthy, but have you ever thought about whether the presents you give reflect this?

I received many sweets and treats from my family when I was a child, but one unlikely gift that I relished was from an eccentric Grandpa. He gave me a children's reference book on sports and fitness. Admittedly not the most typical gift for a wee girl, but it captured my imagination, and I read it over and over again. It's easy to buy someone a box of sweets, but do they really need (or appreciate) them? Here's some ideas of alternative Christmas presents, and remember that simple gifts are usually the ones that are appreciated in the long term.

Children are easy to buy for, try Space hoppers, skipping ropes, bats and balls, hula hoops and skittles (they can never have enough sports equipment to play with). An unexpected winner with a young nephew a couple of years ago was an inexpensive inflatable football goal and ball. A kite is a fun gift, and Edinburgh is certainly windy enough. If the budget allows, a bike or scooter will bring a smile to their face. For older children, sports books that encourage participation are great. The excuse that "the children aren't sporty and would rather a computer game" doesn't wash. Firstly, children can only use active toys if they have them in the first place, and also, it is adults responsibility to set a good example.

Adults may seem trickier, and some folk may worry about offending partners by giving them fitness gifts. My guitar-playing husband appreciated his Powerball ergonomic arm trainer that was a fun way to strengthen grip and arm strength. A Swiss ball or wobble board is a fun gift, as is an adult sized hula hoop from Argos, a brilliant tummy workout. A Wii Fit combines computer games and sport, but is more expensive, especially if it only gets used ever now and again. You're better off buying them a block of personal training sessions so they can learn how to exercise properly.

For foodies, try a healthy eating recipe cookbook, or a good food hamper. Take nicely packaged herbal teas and fancy oatcakes as gifts when visiting friends. Detox teas are particularly appreciated over the festive season.

So use your imagination for some inspirational present-giving, and have a happy and healthy silly season.

## ZZZZZZ (You Are Feeling Sleepy)

Sleep is one of my favourite pastimes over the winter. Personally I sleep more in the darker months and less in the peak of summer. I decided to investigate why we sleep and learnt some very interesting things.

We all know we need to sleep. If we are deprived of sleep our brains behave in very strange ways indeed. I have read reports of people hallucinating after being deprived of sleep for a couple of days. Even depriving yourself of a few extra hours a night can affect your reaction time, memory, attention span, rationality of thinking and give you big dirty bags under your eyes.

You can think of the sleep cycle like a washing machine cycle.

**Part 1:** Light sleep – when you are half asleep and can be awakened easily. You are preparing for a good night's rest and this lasts about 10 minutes

**Part 2:** True sleep – for about 20 minutes your breathing and heart rate slows down as you become disengaged with your surroundings and start to slumber

**Parts 3 & 4:** Deep sleep – Your breathing and heart rate are at their slowest, and your brain starts producing delta waves which are big, slow brain waves. Then…

This is the deepest sleep, where your body is very relaxed and breathing deep and rhythmic. If you are woken from this state it takes a few minutes to adjust to being awake. This is where various hormones are released, our blood pressure drops and our body repairs itself.

Along with these cycles is REM sleep that makes up about 25% of our deep sleep. It's the kind of sleep you see in scary films, where the person's eyes are darting back and forth, and the body is very still. We can think of this as nature's way of recharging our brains and it is the time that much of our dreaming occurs.

Sleep is the time our muscles and body tissue repair themselves from the days' oxidative stress – so if you work out, be sure to get enough sleep so your muscles can repair and rebuild. Sleep also assists our brain in functioning correctly. Our brain function encompasses both the conscious side that we are aware of (i.e. not being groggy), and also such functions as hormone control.

An interesting hormone to consider is cortisol, which is secreted by your adrenal glands, just above your kidneys. Cortisol is produced in a cyclic fashion with the highest levels being released in the morning and the lowest at night. Your cortisol levels help control things like your immune system, your sleeping patterns and how your body burns its fuel. Too much cortisol, and you may experience disturbed REM sleep.

Now, cortisol release is partially dictated by the food you eat. High GI foods that are sugary, processed or high in starch cause a peak in cortisol levels, which in turn can lead to disturbed sleep, fatigue and even weight gain. So, the idea is to keep your cortisol levels as natural as possible, by eating a balanced, low GI diet and getting regular rest. Ideally aim to go to bed at the same time every night, preferably before 11pm and get enough sleep so that you feel well rested.

Eat sensibly, avoiding sugary foods and alcohol in the evening, as they may disturb your sleep. It's also good to have a relaxing evening routine, perhaps read a book or have a bath just before bed. If you find yourself lying in bed worrying about something, get up, and write down the thought on a 'to do' list. Allow yourself to relax and truly enjoy a good night's sleep. Nighty night.

# Acknowledgements

## The Words

The first many of my friends knew of this book was when I sent a message out looking for proofing folk with a few free hours that day as deadline for final copy was within 48 hours. Andy Wright, my lovely husband, not only proofread all of my newsletters and articles over the years, but also this book from cover to cover. Big love also to my dear mother Sue Maxted whose recent visit to Edinburgh started with a proofread of the whole thing. Thanks also to Nina Jones, Alice Parberry, Mark Gillick, Anna Wilkins, Sophie Lockwood and Victoria Neves Pedro all whom proofed a chapter or more.

Edinburgh has been my home for fourteen years now, and is my favourite place in the world. Writing this book has made me truly appreciate how lucky I am to be able to do the job I do, running and cycling around such an awesome city. It's impossible to list all of the people I have met over the years who have inspired me to put together my own book. You know who you are.

Finally big love to my brother David Griffen, a talented food photographer in Cornwall and my father, abstract artist Peter Griffen based in Sydney. They inspired me to believe that anything is possible. Depending on what you want of course.

**Contact Details**

Email: iwantto@getfitandenjoyit.com

Website: www.getfitandenjoyit.com: sign up for your free monthly fitness newsletter

Freephone: 0800 083 5955

Registered office: 3 Balfour Street, Edinburgh, EH6 5BY

Daily fitness & foodie tips on Twitter: www.twitter.com/tracygriffen

Join Griffen Fitness on Facebook: www.facebook.com/griffenfitness

# The Pictures

Once again my right hand man and Zen guru Andy Wright excelled, teaching himself the gentle art of food photography. All recipe photos were styled and photographed by him, and cooked by myself. We ate a number of cold meals in the preparation of this book.

| | |
|---|---|
| Cloud photos | front cover and chapter headings |
| All recipe photos | pages 8, 21, 36, 38, 53, 66, 79, 92, 105, 122, 136, 152, 169 |
| Fruit bowl | page 81 |
| Hooping | page 76 |
| Sushi | page 92 |
| Glenmore forest | page 128 |
| Press up Santa | page 174 |

Contact: andyleftwright@gmail.com

Ian Kinghorn is the genius behind some wonderful illustrations originally published in the Leither magazine 2010 to 2011.

| | |
|---|---|
| Soup cans | page 31 |
| Water lady | page 48 |
| Countryside | page 114 |
| Breathe | page 159 |

Contact: kinghorn73@gmail.com

David Griffen: My brother. He rocks!

| | |
|---|---|
| Bike | page 61 |
| Skipping | page 72 |
| Leaping | page 86 |

Contact: www.davidgriffen.co.uk

Tracy Griffen:

| | |
|---|---|
| Bicycles | page 102 |
| Hill walking | page 143 |

# Index